CW00447362

BY THE SAME AUTHOR

The Identification of British 20th Century Bronze Coin Varieties

BY THE SAME AUTHOR

The Identification of British 20th Century Bronze Coin Varieties

THE IDENTIFICATION OF BRITISH 20th CENTURY SILVER COIN VARIETIES

David J. Groom

The Identification of British 20th Century Silver Coin Varieties

First published in 2010

Text Copyright © David Groom 2010
Cover Design © David Groom 2010

Typeset by DJG,
Whitstable, Kent, United Kingdom
Printed in Great Britain

ISBN: 978-1-4457-5301-0

All rights reserved.

David J. Groom hereby asserts his moral right to be identified as the author of this book.

No part of this publication may be reproduced, stored or introduced into a retrieval system, or transmitted in any form or by any means (electronic, mechanical, photocopying, recording or otherwise) without the prior permission of David J. Groom.

Dedicated to coin collectors everywhere and also to my lovely wife, who is more skilled at spending coins than collecting them, yet who still indulges me in my hobby.

Acknowledgements

This book was conceived from my own confusion over the descriptions of varieties of a number of common coins in different authoritative sources. It was inspired by the discussions and inputs from many of the members of the coin forum at www.predecimal.com and I am grateful to all of those who contribute to this forum and make it such a fascinating place to visit.

In particular, I am grateful to John Henley, one of the members of the above coin forum, for his advice concerning the identification of the 1969 tenpences and kind permission to reproduce photographs of the different types. Also, for his help in providing copies of articles from Coins and Medals magazine from the 1960s and 1970s.

So far as the detailed contents are concerned, my thanks go to Peter J Davies who is the author of the definitive book, 'British Silver Coins Since 1816' for his work in defining the catalogue numbering system used to identify many of the dates, types and varieties I describe in this book.

Finally, it is important to mention a number of lesser known, but vitally important people in the coin world, without whose research and devotion to numismatic duties, many of the details in this book would not be possible. These are the people who, over the decades of the 1970s and 1980s, contributed many research articles to the magazine Coin Monthly on a wide range of aspects of 20th century British coins. They include: A.J.Braybrook, D.H.Perrin, A.W.Bacon, D.M.Beecham, J.C.Rudge, K.B.Wiles, E.B.Mackenzie and R Stafford a group of true numismatists, from whose work I can honestly say that this book of mine was the result of 'standing on the shoulders of giants.'

*   *   *   *   *

CONTENTS   Page

Pre-Decimal Coinage

Victoria

Edward VII

George V

George VI

CONTENTS   Page

Introduction

I have been interested in collecting English coins for most of my adult life, having started in the dying days of pounds, shillings and pence (LSD) in the late 1960s when interesting coins could still be found in everyday change. Like many collectors, I tended to obtain coins by denomination and in date order, eagerly filling gaps in a series as examples became available, including many of the rarer dates. At some point, I became aware that many denominations and dates were produced with minor variations, and I collected a few of these, particularly some of the more well known kinds from the Victorian era. However, I found that there seemed to be an enormous number of them, and collecting them all, even for a specific denomination e.g. farthings, could well become a lifetime's work.

During my collecting career I gradually bought a number of books and magazines concerning coins and coin collecting, and I slowly built up a picture of all the varieties that had been found and were known to exist. Many of these publications, list variants for dates and denominations earlier than the 20th century, but as far as I can judge there is no single definitive book or publication that lists and explains the variants for 20th century coins, including the decimal coinage. Most publications mention some of them and some describe the same varieties in different ways, but I repeat none seems to describe them all in one concise easy to use book.

What this book attempts to do, and readers must make there own minds up about how well I have done so, is to bring together all the information about varieties for all the denominations of silver/cupro-nickel coins (and higher denomination brass i.e. the £1 and £2 coins) minted throughout the 20th century. Many sources exist that quote the characteristics for the varieties of a particular denomination and date, but in many cases those characteristics differ from source to source for the same coin. What I have done in this book is to consider the different descriptions and to reconcile them against examples of a specific type and date. In this way, I hope that a reader who wants to add varieties to their collection of 20th Century silver coins will have a single authoritative reference source to turn to, rather than the many disparate publications that make reference to these different types.

I have included all the issued denominations, including the 'standard' proofs from the sets, but excluded the special proofs and one–off coins that the average collector is unlikely to ever see, let alone be in a position to afford e.g. the 1952 halfcrown. I have also excluded reference to the Maundy series of coins. What I was interested in producing for the collector is a definitive list of all the varieties and a description of exactly what to look for with illustrations of the differences, so that identification of an individual specimen can be quickly established.

Definition and Limitations

Before going any further, I need to define exactly what a variety is so far as this book is concerned, and what limitations this places on the information and descriptions covered. Varieties are usually defined as those coins resulting from deliberate changes to one or both dies of a coin. This may be to correct an error or a weakness in the design, to repair damage to a die or as a result of changes in the production process for a coin.

Varieties can occur anywhere on the design of the coin. They may affect the main features, the border teeth or beads, the legends, the date, the rim, the edge type or inscription, the thickness of the flan, the size and weight, the final finish, etc. In other words, any aspect of a coin as presented may be found to have some sort of variation, which can be compared to coins of the same type and date.

The results of these changes may be to produce coins of a date and denomination with two or more obverse types, two or more reverse types and any combinations of these. It does not follow that because a particular year and denomination has, for example, two obverses and two reverses that this automatically means four varieties. In many cases, a new obverse or reverse die was produced and was used partway through the year for that date and denomination, and then was used in later years leading to just two types in a specific year. These varieties are interesting as they can give insights into the production of coins at the time and a view of some of the problems encountered.

Less significantly, specific types of variety can arise where damage is sustained to a die. For example where a piece of a die breaks off, this will leave a recess and this can lead to a raised area on the coin and weakness of strike elsewhere, which may appear as a change in the design. Conversely, dies may become clogged with extraneous matter and this then leads to parts of the design not being properly struck. Dies can also crack in use, leading to interesting raised features on the surface of a coin, or die clashes may occur, again leading to apparent changes in the design of a coin.

So far as this book is concerned, I have not covered broken dies, die cracks or filled dies in any detail, unless the result is a well known error. Many minor die cracks, clogged dies and other types of error have been discovered over the years, but I have not listed them here, as they are a specialised area in their own right. The exception is those faults which have led to a recognised feature on a coin and were produced in sufficient numbers as to be considered a variety. I accept that many readers may feel that I should either have excluded this specific type of error or conversely included them all. I have some sympathy for this view, but since some of these are regarded conventionally as varieties I have opted to include them. Another error type is the brockage coin, but these are usually one-off coins and again I have not included them since I don't believe they have a place in a book concerning varieties.

The one exception to the above is where damage to a die was spotted and design changes and re-cutting carried out to enable it to continue in use. In this case, there is still a design change, albeit caused by the damage to the die and these varieties have been included in this book, where known. Another type of variety results from processing or striking errors over a period of time, so that the number of pieces may be considerable, and this leads to the type being regarded as a variety rather than an error.

Where a design change has taken place and varieties have been identified, I have classified the resulting coin types as major varieties. Where the design changes are small, perhaps as a result of re-cutting following die damage or where the type has gathered sufficient notoriety or support from collectors as to be regarded as a variety, I have generally classified these as minor varieties. Broadly speaking, I have provided photographs of the distinguishing features of just about every major type, so that readers can quickly spot the design changes that took place, leading them to easily identify coins in their collections or which they buy.

Whilst researching this book, I came across an extraordinary design issue, which I had never heard of before, but which can be regarded as leading to micro-varieties (as if minor types are not enough!). In the Coin Monthly magazine of December 1977, there is an article by J.C.Rudge entitled 'The 19 Varieties of the 1949 Shilling', which talks about the successful prosecution of a Mr. James Steele of Edinburgh. This individual was found guilty of forging excellent quality florins, in part at least, because the Royal Mint were able to show that his coins, whilst superbly forged, had errors in the number of 'nicks' in the edge milling. Apparently, the Mint declined to provide information about this means of validating their coins on security grounds, suggesting that the number of nicks could be regarded as a kind of 'mint mark' in order to validate the year they were produced. In a feat of truly heroic study, J.C.Rudge set about analysing these nicks for the silver series i.e. the sixpence, shilling, florin and halfcrown (I'm not sure about crowns), publishing his results in the British Numismatic Journal for 1968. The 1977 Coin Monthly article concluded that the 1949 Shilling has at least 19 varieties based on the number of edge nicks. Multiply this typical figure by all the silver coin denominations and dates for the 20th Century and the number of micro-varieties based on the number of 'nicks' will be truly staggering. Having said this, I cannot believe that even the most pedantic anorak of a collector would set about basing their collection on this factor. For this reason, I have deliberately not included these coins in this book. However, readers who want to know more should consult the articles in Coin Monthly, references to which are contained in appendix 2.

For the old pre-decimal coinage, which was demonetised on D-day on 15th February 1971, there were many detailed studies carried out in the dying days of the old currency and through the 1970s and 1980s, which examined many examples of the various dates and denominations of coins struck during the 20th century. These studies, which were reported in coin publications at the time, investigated possible varieties of 20th century coins, the results of which showed many very minor, almost imperceptible changes in design. Where identified, I have included the specific details of these minor varieties in this book, and where possible I have provided photographs to enable the reader to differentiate each of the types.

The one thing this book does not do is detail the history of the coins and the numismatic reasons for the variety. The aim is very clear: to provide a reference point for collectors, to enable them to quickly identify the varieties they have in their collections and to enable them to easily identify new examples when out at coin fairs, antique shows, shops, boot fairs, auctions etc. This book is written, not for the investor or the casual reader, but for the serious collector, who is interested in 20th century varieties and wants a single reference source to use in the hunt for them in order to enhance his or her collection.

3

Collecting

Many of the varieties described in this book are not specifically identified by dealers or auctioneers, but may be readily found if you know what to look for. It is also the case that many of them are varieties of common, relatively modern coins of the last 60-70 years, but they are rarely advertised by dealers as the margins are too small and they can often only be found by a good rummage through a dealer's trays, or in the pots and tins at a boot fair. For this reason these varieties can be quite hard to find because the basic date and denomination itself is rarely specifically offered for sale, and it can, therefore, be difficult to find examples of some of them without considerable effort.

Occasionally, particularly on internet auction sites, dealers do take the trouble to identify specific varieties for a coin. However, this is usually only for the rarer types, where there is the possibility for increased profit. Nevertheless, the internet is a useful source for obtaining varieties for a collection, particularly if the seller puts up good quality photographs of the coin for sale. Unfortunately, many do not, especially for common dates and denominations and again this makes for difficulties in finding them.

Where decimal coins are concerned, many of these are still in circulation and examples can be plucked from change, albeit in worn condition. However, top quality examples will again be hard to find as dealers rarely carry extensive stock of even the withdrawn types of decimal coinage e.g. the early large 5p, 10p and 50p, so finding varieties of these can prove difficult.

Book Structure

In this book, I have catalogued the varieties by reign in the first instance, starting in 1900 with Queen Victoria through to the decimal coinage of Queen Elizabeth II in 1999, with subsequent sub-divisions into the different denominations, thus following the traditions of most other numismatic books. I only describe the standard coin and its variants for a specific date and where no variant is known, then that date is not described for that denomination.

However, all denominations are mentioned and where no varieties exist or have been reported then this is recorded. Thus this book covers both the positive identification of the varieties, but also includes positive statements about the non-existence of varieties for a particular denomination. In this way, readers can be assured that all coins were considered and researched and there should be no ambiguity or doubt about the status of any denomination or date.

Throughout this book, I have used Peter J Davies' excellent book, 'British Silver Coins Since 1816' as the defining source for the major varieties, as this is the source most often used by dealers when identifying and quoting catalogue numbers of silver coins for sale.

Where necessary, I have consulted other well known standard books on coins, but have also considered other publications and sources where varieties are identified. I have tried to include every variety that I have come across in order to make sure the book is comprehensive and, where different sources define the varieties by different characteristics, I have tried to reconcile the descriptions. In this way I hope that the user of this book will have a single definitive source on which to base decisions about his or her collection.

Virtually all of the photographs in this book are taken from coins that I have owned or have in my collection. In a few cases I have been unable to find a piece (usually the rarities) and I have had to reconcile descriptions in different books without a specimen in front of me. In doing so I accept blindly that the variety actually exists and has been seen by somebody at some time. Occasionally, I have come across references to varieties without an adequate description of the distinguishing features. In these case, I have included what little is known, and I leave it to the reader to carry out their own further research to see if they can establish what the differences are.

In a few cases, the sources I have used provide multiple descriptions of the features for a particular variety. I have made reference to these descriptions throughout the book, but where I have provided photographs, I have generally only included examples where the features that distinguish the varieties are clear to the eye, or perhaps through a magnifying glass. Where there are matters of minute measurement e.g. a difference in size of say 0.2mm, then I have generally not included photographs and I have recommended identifying the variety by other more readily understood means, where possible.

New Varieties

This book can only include the known varieties at the time of writing, and you can be sure that the moment this is published, a dozen or so new ones will be discovered. I think this is another manifestation of 'Murphy's Law'. If not it's certainly related to the law that says toast always lands jam-side down!

New varieties are perhaps less likely for the pre-decimal series, as these were well researched during the years leading up to and just after decimalisation in 1971, when there were huge numbers of coins available for study. However, for decimal coins, some varieties have been reported for the earlier years, and are included here, but I have been able to find little information about more recent dates and whether varieties exist for them. It may be that production methods and quality control mean that there are few, if any, to find. More likely, perhaps there has been little effort made to study a large enough sample of coins to establish the differences.

Anyway, if any readers are, or become aware of, any new varieties that need to be included, please let me know, preferably with pictures so that I can include them in any future revised edition of this book. My contact details and email address are at the back of this book in appendix 1. Appropriate acknowledgements will be given, thus immortalising the sender in print. Similarly, this book also acknowledges the inputs made from a number of sources in the coin collecting/publishing world, a full bibliographical list of whom is at appendix 2. If anybody has been missed then I apologise humbly, and will put this right with the next edition.

Sources

As I have said earlier, for silver coins, the key source for data was Davies, but additional information came from Salzman, Coins Market Values publications and the Rotographic publications, Collector's Coins GB 2007, (and earlier dates), Check Your Change, plus the magazine Coin Monthly, which, in the 1970s and 80s, provided many informative articles about the minor varieties of the silver coinage. The larger denomination decimal brass £1 and £2 coins are also included, again with inputs from additional sources.

Bronze coins and their varieties, including the brass threepence, are described in 'The Identification of British 20th Century Bronze Coin Varieties,' which is a sister edition of this book. The only types not covered in either book are gold. These are described in detail by Michael A Marsh, but as far as I can judge none of the other source documents list any varieties for gold, in which case, Marsh must be regarded as the single authoritative source. I am aware of some varieties for certain denominations e.g. the Proof 1937 £5 piece, but I do not believe that there are sufficient types overall, as to justify a separate book covering gold in its own right. Also, there are not likely to be too many variety collectors for these coins. For these two reasons, therefore, I have no intention of producing a similar book covering the gold coinage of the 20th century.

The above sources leave out three important numismatic publications: Spink, ESC and Coincraft. Whilst Spink's 'Coins of England' is one of the best known and valuable annually published books for identifying and pricing coins, it does not attempt to describe all of the varieties of the coins it lists. Only a few very well-known ones are mentioned e.g. the 1926 halfcrown missing the colon after OMN, and for this reason, I have not quoted the Spink numbering scheme in this book.

'The English Silver coinage From 1649' by H A Seaby and P A Rayner or ESC for short, is also a defining publication concerning English silver coinage, but like Spink it does not cover varieties in any detail, and so I have not made use of the ESC numbering scheme here. However, it does give estimates of rarity for the various dates, which will obviously have a bearing on the consequent rarity of varieties, particularly for the scarcer dates.

Finally, the publication, 'Coincraft's 1997 Catalogue of English & UK Coins 1066 to Date' is a treasure trove of information and pictures of coins going back to 1066, again with prices. This book does mention varieties under each denomination and reign but unfortunately does not specify or illustrate the types, so again, I do not make reference to this book's numbering scheme here.

The other source of data consulted during the writing of this book is the internet. Coin dealer's websites, eBay and a number of other informative websites were all consulted for details of varieties. However, most numismatic web sites either trade in coins or describe the main types by denomination or reign, or both. Few make very much effort to describe or consistently differentiate between types for the reasons I have given above. The one exception is that of Michael Gouby at http://www.michael-coins.co.uk/. This site not only lists a great many coins for sale, but also comprehensively distinguishes many varieties by reference to clear identifying features and photographs.

A full bibliography of sources is given at the back of this book at appendix 2.

Rarity

In this book I give no mathematical indication of rarity as I have been unable to study a large enough sample to gauge this, although I do comment on the perceived rarity according to the sources I have used.

Values

Many of the references consulted in the preparation of this book are annual publications which contain up to date information about values of coins. Anybody who wishes to establish a valuation of their collection, including varieties should consult the latest versions of these books or seek the advice of a professional coin dealer. In this book I have refrained from giving any indication of values according to grade, partly because I have insufficient data, but also because such prices are subject to the whims of the market and can change rapidly. Having said this, many of the varieties are not distinguished by dealers and there is, therefore, no differentiation of price between them. However, in some cases, specific varieties are identified and, where rare, dealer's prices do usually reflect this.

Coin Collectors

One final thought: many groups have a collective term e.g. a parliament of owls, a murder of crows, a rabble of butterflies or a glean of herrings. Whilst not in any way suggesting that numismatists are in the same category as animals, insects, fish or birds, I wonder if a 'variety' of coin collectors would fit the bill (no bird pun intended). After all, we come in all shapes and sizes and collect a wide range of denominations, types and countries, so variety seems most appropriate.

And so to the varieties!

*   *   *   *   *

PRE-DECIMAL COINAGE

Victoria

Period: 1838 – 1901

Denomination: Threepence

1895 – 1901

Specification: Diameter: 16mm
Weight: 1.4g
Metal: Silver (92.5%)

Obverse Design:

Victoria's veiled head bust facing left with abbreviated legend as follows:

'VICTORIA·DEI·GRA·BRITT·REGINA·FID·DEF·IND·IMP·' – 1895 to 1901

Reverse Design:

A crowned '3' dividing the date, all within a wreath.

Edge: Plain

Years Produced: 1893 – 1901 inclusive, with a proof in 1893.

Varieties:

Only two dates fall within the 20th Century and there are no identified design varieties for either the obverse or reverse.

*   *   *   *   *

Denomination: Sixpence

1893 – 1901

Specification: Diameter: 19mm
Weight: 3.0g
Metal: Silver (92.5%)

Obverse Design:

Victoria's veiled head bust facing left with abbreviated legend as follows:

'VICTORIA·DEI·GRA·BRITT·REGINA·FID·DEF·IND·IMP·' – 1893 to 1901

Reverse Design:

'SIX PENCE' in words on two lines, across the centre, with crown above and surrounded by a wreath and the date below.

Edge: Milled

Years Produced: 1895 – 1901 inclusive, with a proof in 1893.

Varieties:

For the two dates which fall within the 20th Century, no varieties have been described, either for the obverse or reverse.

*   *   *   *   *

Denomination: Shilling

1993 – 1901

Specification: Diameter: 24mm
Weight: 5.7g
Metal: Silver (92.5%)

Obverse Design:

Victoria's veiled head bust facing left with abbreviated legend as follows:

'VICTORIA·DEI·GRA·BRITT·REGINA·FID·DEF·IND·IMP·' – 1893 to 1901

Reverse Design:

Three shields arranged in an inverted triangle within a garter, with the inscription 'HONI SOIT QUI MAL Y PENSE' on the garter, but partially hidden by the shields. The words 'ONE SHILLING' around the outside of the garter on the upper part of the coin and the date in the lower part.

Edge: Milled

Years Produced: 1893 – 1901 inclusive, again with a proof in 1893.

Varieties:

For the two dates which fall within the 20th Century, there are no varieties for either of them.

*   *   *   *   *

Denomination: Florin

1893 – 1901

Specification: Diameter: 28.5mm
Weight: 11.3g
Metal: Silver (92.5%)

Obverse Design:

Victoria's veiled head bust facing left with abbreviated legend as follows:

'VICTORIA·DEI·GRA·BRITT·REGINA·FID·DEF·IND·IMP·' – 1893 to 1901

Reverse Design:

Three shields with crown above, arranged in an inverted triangle and separated by a rose, shamrock and thistle within a garter, with the inscription 'HONI SOIT QUI MAL Y PENSE' on the garter, but partially hidden by the shields. The words 'ONE FLORIN' around the outside of the garter on the left hand side and the words 'TWO SHILLINGS' on the right hand side. The date lies below the garter at the bottom of the coin.

Edge: Milled

Years Produced: 1893 – 1901 inclusive, with a proof in 1893.

Varieties:

For the two dates which fall within the 20th Century, there are no varieties for either date.

*   *   *   *   *

Denomination: Halfcrown

1893 – 1901

Specification: Diameter: 32mm
                        Weight:14.1g
                        Metal: Silver (92.5%)

Obverse Design:

Victoria's veiled head bust facing left with abbreviated legend as follows:

'VICTORIA·DEI GRA·BRITT·REG·' – 1893 to 1901

Reverse Design:

A crowned spade shaped shield in the collar of the garter and the legend 'FID·DEF·IND·IMP' around the top half of the coin and '· HALF CROWN· ' around the bottom, separated by the date.

Edge: Milled

Years Produced: 1893 – 1901 inclusive, with a proof in 1893.

Varieties:

For the two dates which fall within the 20th Century, there are no varieties for either date.

*   *   *   *   *

Denomination: Crown

1893 – 1900

Specification: Diameter: 39mm
Weight: 28.3g
Metal: Silver (92.5%)

Obverse Design:

Victoria's veiled head bust facing left with abbreviated legend as follows:

'VICTORIA·DEI·GRA·BRITT·REGINA·FID·DEF·IND·IMP·' – 1893 to 1900

Reverse Design:

Pistrucci's St George and the dragon design with the date in the exergue.

Edge: In relief inscription 'DECUS ET TUTAMEN ANNO REGNI' followed by the regnal date in roman numerals. The inscription is upright in relation to the obverse.

Years Produced: 1893 – 1900 inclusive, with a proof in 1893. None were produced in 1901, the last year of Victoria's reign.

Varieties:

For the single date which falls within the 20th Century, there are two major varieties based on the edge inscription and minor varieties for one of these.

1900 Crown:

Major Varieties:

There are two major varieties distinguished by the regnal year found on the edge. These are LXIII and LXIV and the two edge inscriptions read:

1. DECUS ET TUTAMEN ANNO REGNI LXIII – Davies 532 or 533
2. DECUS ET TUTAMEN ANNO REGNI LXIV – Davies 534

13

Minor Varieties:

There are two minor varieties of the 1900 LXIII crown. They can be distinguished by the distance from the lettering to the border teeth on the obverse, which can be either wide or narrow, classified by Davies with numbers 533 and 532 respectively. Of the two, the narrow gap type is rarer.

Figure 1 – 1900 LXIII Crown Obverses

Wider gap – legend to teeth   Narrow gap – legend to teeth

There are also reports of a few specimens with the edge inscription upside down.

*   *   *   *   *

Edward VII

Period: 1902 – 1910

Denomination: Threepence

1902 – 1910

Specification: Diameter: 16mm
Weight: 1.4g
Metal: Silver (92.5%)

Obverse Design:

Edward's bust facing right with abbreviated legend as follows:

'EDWARDVS VII D:G:BRITT:OMN:REX F:D:IND:IMP:' – 1902 to 1910

Reverse Design:

A crowned '3' which divides the date within a wreath.

Edge: Plain

Years Produced: 1902 - 1910 only and with a matt proof in the sets of 1902.

Varieties:

Major Varieties have been reported for three years of this reign: 1904, 1905 and 1906, but no minor varieties have been reported for the series.

1904 Threepence:

Major Varieties:

There are four varieties of the 1904 threepence, based on two obverses (obverses 1 and 2) and two reverses (reverses A and B), giving the combinations 1+A, 1+B, 2+A and 2+B. Davies catalogues these as numbers: 1592, 1593, 1594 and 1595, respectively.

Obverses:

Obverse 1: Obverse 1 of the 1904 threepence has several key identifiers that distinguish it from Obverse 2:

- A wide gap between the colon after 'IND' and the 'I' of 'IMP'.
- The 'I' of 'IMP' points to a bead.
- The colon after 'IND' points to a border bead.
- The right upright of the 'N' in 'OMN' points to a space.
- The 'I' of 'BRITT' points to a space.
- There are 129 border teeth.

Obverse 2: For obverse 2 there are key differences:

- A narrower gap between the colon after 'IND' and the 'I' of 'IMP'.
- The 'I' of 'IMP' points to a space.
- The colon after 'IND' points to a space.
- The right upright of the 'N' in 'OMN' points to a border bead.
- The 'I' of 'BRITT' points to a border tooth.
- There are 122 border teeth.

Counting border teeth isn't the easiest of tasks and this method is not recommended as a means of identification.

Figure 2 – 1904 Threepence Obverses (1)

Obverse 1	**Obverse 2**
Wide gap colon to 'I'	Narrow gap colon to 'I'
Colon to a bead	Colon to a space
'I' to a bead	'I' to a space.

Figure 3 – 1904 Threepence Obverses (2)

Obverse 1	**Obverse 2**
Right Leg of 'N' to a space	Right leg of 'N' to a bead

16

Figure 4 – 1904 Threepence Obverses (3)

Obverse 1
'I' to space

Obverse 2
'I' to bead

Reverses:

Reverse A: This reverse is found on threepences with dates from 1902 to 1904:

- The '3' has a small ball on the end of the lower tail.
- The base of the '3' is further from the bow of the ribbon than on reverse B.
- The '3' has a longer neck or diagonal stroke.
- The top of the '3' is away from the crown.
- The top of the upper loop of the '3' is highly arched.

Reverse B: This reverse is found on coins from 1904 to 1910 and differs from reverse A in several key ways:

- The '3' has a larger ball on the end of the lower tail.
- The base of the '3' is closer to the bow of the ribbon than on reverse A.
- The '3' has a shorter neck or diagonal stroke.
- The top of the '3' is closer to the crown.
- The top of the upper loop of the '3' is less arched.

Figure 5 – 1904 Threepence Reverses (1)

Reverse A
Small Ball
Large gap to ribbon

Reverse B
Larger Ball
Small gap to ribbon

Figure 6 – 1904 Threepence Reverses (2)

Reverse A	Reverse B
Longer neck to '3'	Shorter neck to '3'
Top of '3' away from crown	Top of '3' close to crown
Highly arched lower loop	Less arched lower loop

Minor Varieties:

There are no reported minor varieties for this date and denomination.

1905 Threepence:

Major Varieties:

There are two varieties of the 1905 threepence, based on two obverses (obverses 1 and 2) and a single reverse (reverse B), giving the combinations 1+B and 2+B. Davies catalogues these as numbers: 1596 and 1597 respectively, although the former is catalogued as unconfirmed. It has been suggested that obverse 1 is only found on the Maundy series and that worn specimens found with this obverse are merely Maundy pieces that have been put into circulation.

Obverses 1 and 2 for the 1905 threepence are identical to those for 1904 and the details are shown in figures 2 – 4.

Minor Varieties:

No minor varieties have been reported for this date and denomination.

1906 Threepence:

Major Varieties:

As for 1905, there are two varieties of the 1906 threepence, based on two obverses (obverses 1 and 2) and a single reverse (reverse B), giving the combinations 1+B and 2+B. Davies catalogues these as numbers: 1598 and 1599 respectively.

Obverses 1 and 2 for the 1906 threepence are identical to those for 1904 and 1905 and the details can be seen figures 2 – 4.

Minor Varieties:

No minor varieties have been reported for this date and denomination.

*   *   *   *   *

Denomination: Sixpence

1902 – 1910

Specification: Diameter: 19mm
Weight: 3.0g
Metal: Silver (92.5%)

Obverse Design:

Edward's bust facing right with abbreviated legend as follows:

'EDWARDVS VII DEI GRA:BRITT:OMN:REX FID:DEF:IND:IMP:'

– 1902 to 1910

Reverse Design:

The word 'SIX' above 'PENCE' within a wreath, with a crown above and date below.

Edge: Milled.

Years Produced: 1902 – 1910 inclusive, plus a matt proof in the 1902 sets.

Varieties:

For this date run there are no reported varieties.

*   *   *   *   *

20

Denomination: Shilling

1902 – 1910

Specification: Diameter: 24mm
                     Weight: 5.7g
                     Metal: Silver (92.5%)

Obverse Design:

Edward's bust facing right with abbreviated legend as follows:

'EDWARDVS VII DEI GRA:BRITT:OMN:REX' – 1902 to 1910

Reverse Design:

A lion statant, facing the front on top of a crown, which separates the date. All within an inner circle with the words 'FID: DEF: IND: IMP:' around the top half of the coin and 'ONE SHILLING' around the bottom.

Edge: Milled.

Years Produced: 1902 – 1910 inclusive, with a matt proof in the 1902 sets.

Varieties:

For this date run there are reported major varieties for 1904, 1905 and 1906, all based around differences in the obverse design and a minor variety for 1903. The major varieties are described and catalogued by Davies, but not the 1903 minor variety. Also, there are minor varieties identified for dates from 1907 to 1910.

1903 Shilling:

Major Varieties:

There are no reported major varieties for this date.

Minor Varieties:

The 1903 shilling is found with two obverses (obverses 1 and 2a) and with a single reverse (reverse A) giving the varieties 1+A and 2a+A. According to Davies, Obverse 1 is found on coins dated from 1902 – 1906, whilst obverse 2 is found on all coins from 1904 -1910. Obverse 2a is not described by Davies but has been found on coins dated 1903, 1904 and 1906.

21

1904 Shilling:

Major Varieties:

The 1904 shilling is found with three obverses (obverses 1, 2 and 2a) and with a single reverse (reverse A), giving die pairings 1+A, 2+A and 2a+A.

Minor Varieties:

There are no reported minor varieties for this date.

1905 Shilling:

Major Varieties:

The 1905 shilling has major varieties 1+A and 2+A, with the 2+A being the common type, if 'common' is a term that can be used for a scarce date.

Minor Varieties:

There are no reported minor varieties for this date.

1906 Shilling:

Major Varieties:

Like the 1904 year, three minor varieties for this year have been identified: 1+A, 2+A and 2a+A.

Minor Varieties:

There are no reported major varieties for this date.

Obverses: All Years

Obverse 1:

- The line of the base of 'TT' projects above the base of the 'I', both in 'BRITT'.
- The top bars of the 'TT' are perfectly aligned.
- The upper colon dot after the 'T' in 'BRITT' lies below the bar of the 'T'.
- The tail of the 'R' in 'BRITT' is curved and aligns with the 'I' of 'BRITT'.
- The 'R' and 'I' of 'BRITT' have a small space between them.
- The 'E' of 'DEI' has a long upper arm.
- The 'E' of 'EDWARDVS' is long and the same length as the bottom arm.
- The tail of the 'R' in 'EDWARDVS' is curved, long and aligns with the 'D'.
- There is a small gap between the tail of the 'R' and the 'D' in 'EDWARDVS'.
- The right foot of the 'A' in 'EDWARDVS' is wide.
- The second 'D' in 'EDWARDVS' is large and close to the rim.

- The tail of the 'R' in 'GRA' is curved and aligns with the foot of the 'A'.
- The right foot of the 'A' in 'GRA' is wide.
- The right edge of the top of the 'G' in 'GRA' is slanted back wards.
- The 'E' of 'REX' has a long upper bar.
- The 'R' of 'REX' is curved and its tip has a small gap to the 'E'.

Obverse 2:

- The line of the base of 'TT' projects below the base of the 'I', both in 'BRITT'.
- The top bars of the 'TT' are slightly misaligned, with the right hand one pointing above the left.
- The upper colon dot after the 'T' in 'BRITT' aligns with the bar of the 'T'.
- The tail of the 'R' in 'BRITT' is slightly curved and is below the 'I' of 'BRITT'.
- The 'R' and 'I' of 'BRITT' have a small space between them.
- The 'E' of 'DEI' has a short upper arm.
- The 'E' of 'EDWARDVS' is shorter than the bottom arm.
- The tail of the 'R' in 'EDWARDVS' is curved, longer and lies below the line of the 'D'.
- There is a small gap between the tail of the 'R' and the 'D' in 'EDWARDVS'.
- The right foot of the 'A' in 'EDWARDVS' is narrower.
- The second 'D' in 'EDWARDVS' is smaller and away from the rim.
- The tail of the 'R' in 'GRA' is straighter and the tip lies slightly below the foot of the 'A'.
- The right foot of the 'A' in 'GRA' is narrower.
- The right edge of the top of the 'G' in 'GRA' is more upright.
- The 'E' of 'REX' has a shorter upper bar.
- The tail of the 'R' of 'REX' is straight and its tip has a wider gap to the 'E'.

Obverse 2a:

- The line of the base of 'TT' projects below the base of the 'I', both in 'BRITT'.
- The top bars of the 'TT' are slightly misaligned, with the right hand one pointing above the left.
- The upper colon dot after the 'T' in 'BRITT' aligns with the bar of the 'T'.
- The tail of the 'R' in 'BRITT' is straight and the tip is below the 'I' of 'BRITT'.
- The 'R' and 'I' of 'BRITT' have a wider space between them.
- The 'E' of 'DEI' has a short upper arm.
- The 'E' of 'EDWARDVS' is shorter than the bottom arm.
- The tail of the 'R' in 'EDWARDVS' is straight, shorter and below the line of the 'D'.
- There is a wide gap between the tail of the 'R' and the 'D' in 'EDWARDVS'.
- The right foot of the 'A' in 'EDWARDVS' is narrower.
- The second 'D' in 'EDWARDVS' is smaller and away from the rim.
- The tail of the 'R' in 'GRA' is straighter and the tip lies slightly below the foot of the 'A'.
- The right foot of the 'A' in 'GRA' is narrower.
- The right edge of the top of the 'G' in 'GRA' is slanted back wards slightly.

- The 'E' of 'REX' has a shorter upper bar.
- The tail of the 'R' of 'REX' is straight and its tip has a wider gap to the 'E'.

Obverse 2a is a comparatively recent discovery and for this reason is not identified by any of the well known cataloguers, including Davies.

Figure 7 – Edward VII Shilling Obverses (1)

Obverse 1	**Obverses 2 & 2a**
Base line of 'TT' above base of 'I'	Base line of 'TT' below base of 'I'
Alignment of top bars of 'TT'	Misalignment of top bars of 'TT'
Low upper colon dot	Aligned upper colon dot

Figure 8 – Edward VII Shilling Obverses (2)

Obverses 1	**Obverse 2**	**Obverse 2a**
Curved tip of leg of 'R'	Curved tip of leg of 'R'	Straight leg to the 'R'
'R' leg aligns with 'I'	'R' leg below the 'I'	'R' leg below the 'I'
Small gap 'R' to 'I'	Small gap 'R' to 'I'	Larger gap 'R' to 'I'

Figure 9 – Edward VII Shilling Obverses (3)

Obverse 1	**Obverses 2 & 2a**
Long upper arm to 'E'	Shorter upper arm to 'E'

Figure 10 – Edward VII Shilling Obverses (4)

Obverse 1
Upper arm of 'E' equals lower arm
Tail of 'R is curved
Tail of the 'R' is long
Tail of the 'R' aligns with 'D'
Small gap 'R' to 'D'
Wide right foot of 'A'
Second 'D' is large
Second 'D' is close to rim

Obverse 2a
Upper arm of 'E' shorter than lower arm
Tail of 'R' is straight
Tail of 'R' is short
Tail of 'R' below base of 'D'
Wide gap 'R' to 'D'
Narrower right foot to 'A'
Second 'D' is small
Second 'D' is away from rim

Obverse 2
Upper arm of 'E' shorter than lower arm
Tail of 'R' is curved
Tail of 'R' is long
Tail of 'R' below base of 'D'
Small gap 'R' to 'D'
Narrower right foot to 'A'
Second 'D' is small
Second 'D' away from rim

Figure 11 – Edward VII Shilling Obverses (5)

Obverse 1
Curved leg to the 'R'
'R' aligns with foot of 'A'
Right foot of the 'A' is wide
Top edge of 'G' slopes backwards

Obverses 2 & 2a
Straight leg to the 'R'
'R' below foot of 'A'
Right foot of the 'A is narrow
Top edge of 'G' more upright

25

Figure 12 – Edward VII Shilling Obverses (6)

Obverse 1
Upper arm of 'E' equals lower arm
Tail of 'R is curved
Small gap tail of 'R' to 'E'

Obverse 2 & 2a
Upper arm of 'E' shorter than lower arm
Tail of 'R' is straight
Wide gap tail of 'R' to 'E'

1907 to 1910 Shillings:

Davies and the other data sources all agree that there are no major or minor varieties of the shillings in this part of the date series, with all coins having obverse 2. However, close examination shows that there are a number of minor differences between the designs in each of these years.

These differences revolve around the shape of the legs of the 'Rs' in 'EDWARDVS' and 'BRITT'. In each case, the tips of the legs can be either curved or straight. The following combinations have been noted, where the first descriptor is the 'R' in 'EDWARDVS' and the second is the 'R' in 'BRITT':

1907 – Curved, curved
        Straight, straight
        Straight, curved

1908 – Straight, straight
        Straight, curved

1909 – Curved, curved
        Curved, straight
        Straight, straight

1910 – Curved, straight
        Straight, straight

Given a larger sample of examples to study, it may be that there are other combinations to be found. Furthermore, these known combinations suggest the existence of obverse 2 and 2a varieties for some of the dates, but certain combinations also suggest new varieties, which are a hybrid of these two. A subject area for further study, perhaps?

*   *   *   *   *

Denomination: Florin

1902 – 1910

Specification: Diameter: 28.5mm
Weight: 11.3g
Metal: Silver (92.5%)

Obverse Design:

Edward's bust facing right with abbreviated legend as follows:

'EDWARDVS VII D: G: BRITT: OMN: REX F: D: IND: IMP:' – 1902 to 1910

Reverse Design:

Britannia, standing on a stylised boat, with a shield and spear, inside an open inner ring. The words 'ONE FLORIN' around the left hand side and 'TWO SHILLINGS' around the right, with the date below.

Edge: Milled.

Years Produced: 1902 – 1910 inclusive, again with a matt proof in the 1902 sets.

Varieties:

For this date run there are no reported varieties.

*   *   *   *   *

27

Denomination: Halfcrown

1902 – 1910

Specification: Diameter: 32mm
Weight: 14.1g
Metal: Silver (92.5%)

Obverse Design:

Edward's bust facing right with abbreviated legend as follows:

'EDWARDVS VII DEI GRA: BRITT: OMN: REX' – 1902 to 1910

Reverse Design:

A crowned shield within a garter. Around the top of the garter, the inscription: 'FID: DEF: IND: IMP:' and around the bottom the word 'HALF CROWN' divided by the date.

The garter itself has the inscription 'HONI SOIT QUI' to the left and 'MAL Y PENSE' on the right, on both sides slightly obscured by the shield.

Edge: Milled.

Years Produced: 1902 – 1910 inclusive, with a matt proof in the sets of 1902.

Varieties:

For this date run there are no reported varieties.

*   *   *   *   *

Denomination: Crown

1902

Specification: Diameter: 39mm
Weight: 28.3g
Metal: Silver (92.5%)

Obverse Design:

Edward's bust facing right with abbreviated legend as follows:

'EDWARDVS VII DEI GRA: BRITT: OMN: REX FID: DEF: IND: IMP:' – 1902

Reverse Design:

Pistrucci's iconic St George and the dragon design, with the date in the exergue below.

Edge: Inscribed in relief 'DECUS ET TUTAMEN ANNO REGNI II' and upright when the coin is face up.

Years Produced: 1902 only business strike plus a matt proof strike from the sets.

Varieties:

For this coin there are no specified design varieties, although there are reports of variations in the width of the edge regnal date (II).

*   *   *   *   *

George V

Period: 1911 – 1936

Denomination: Threepence

1911 – 1926 (including the modified effigy)

1927 (proof) – 1936

Specification: Diameter: 16mm
Weight: 1.4g
Metal: Silver (92.5%) 1911 to 1920
(50%) 1920 to 1936

Obverse Design:

George's bust facing left with abbreviated legend as follows:

'GEORGIVS V D.G.BRITT:OMN:REX F.D.IND:IMP:' – 1911 to 1936

Reverse Design:

1. A crowned '3' which divides the date within a wreath – 1911 to 1926.

2. Three oak sprigs each with an acorn attached. The design has a 'G' at the centre and the words 'THREE PENCE' and the date spaced equally round the coin – 1927 to 1936.

Edge: Plain

Years Produced: 1911 to 1936, excepting 1923, 1924, 1927 and 1929 for the business strike, plus proofs in the sets of 1911 and 1927.

Varieties:

Major varieties are found for the years 1911, 1914, 1920 and 1926, with minor varieties in the years 1919, 1921 and 1922. There are no reported varieties for the 'acorn' design between 1927 and 1936.

30

1911 Business Strike Threepence:

Major Varieties:

There are four varieties of the 1911 threepence, which has two obverses (obverses 1 and 2) and two reverses (reverses A and B), giving the die pairings 1+A, 2+A, 1+B, and 2+B. Davies describes all four types, cataloguing them as numbers 1920, 1921, 1922 and 1923 whilst other sources only differentiate the two obverses.

Obverses:

Obverse 1: There are several very obvious identifiers for this obverse:

- The 'I' of 'BRITT' points to a border bead.
- The 'I' of 'GEORGIVS' points to a border bead.
- The king's head is 'hollow.' This is the well known hollow neck variety.
- There are 121 border beads.

Obverse 2: This type is identified by:

- The 'I' of 'BRITT' points to a space between border beads.
- The 'I' of 'GEORGIVS' points to the right of a bead and into the space.
- The king's head is 'smooth.' This is the so-called flat neck type.
- There are 122 border beads.

Counting border beads is the least simple way to differentiate these two types.

Figure 13 – 1911 Threepence Obverses (1)

Obverse 1	**Obverse 2**
'I' in 'BRITT' points to a bead	'I' in 'BRITT' points to a space

Figure 14 – 1911 Threepence Obverses (2)

Obverse 1	**Obverse 2**
'I' in 'GEORGIVS' points to a bead	'I' in 'GEORGIVS' points to right of bead

Figure 15 – 1911 Threepence Obverses (3)

Obverse 1
Hollow Neck

Obverse 2
Flat Neck

Reverses:

Reverse A: There are three minor differentiators for this type:

- The top leaf on the left hand side has a cone shaped base.
- The top left hand stalk runs straight to the leaf.
- The leaf connects to the leaf axel.

Reverse B:

- The top leaf on the left hand side is shorter and not cone shaped.
- The top left hand stalk is bent to the leaf.
- The leaf connects to the left hand berry stem.

Figure 16 – 1911 Threepence Reverses

Reverse A
Cone shaped base to leaf
Longer leaf
Stalk straight to leaf
Leaf connects to axel

Reverse B
Leaf not cone shaped.
Shorter leaf.
Stalk bends to leaf
Leaf connects to berry stem

Minor Varieties:

There are no reported minor varieties for this date.

1914 Threepence:

Major Varieties:

There are two varieties of the 1914 threepence which has two obverses (obverses 2 and 3) and a single reverse (reverse B), giving the die pairings 2+B and 3+B. Davies describes both types, cataloguing them with numbers 1926 and 1927, as do several other sources.

Obverses:

Obverse 2:

- The 'I' in 'GEORGIVS' points to the right of a border bead.
- The 'P' in 'IMP' points to a border bead.
- The 'D' in 'FD' points to a space between beads.
- There are 122 border teeth.

Obverse 3:

- The 'I' in 'GEORGIVS' points to the left of a border bead.
- The 'P' of 'IMP' points to a space between two beads.
- The 'D' in 'FD' points to a bead.
- There are 120 border teeth.

There are conflicting reports about the pointing of the 'I' in 'GEORGIVS'. This is described by Davies as to the left of a bead for obverse 3 and to the right of a border bead for obverse 2. Other sources define these as to a bead for obverse 3 and to a space between beads for obverse 2. On balance, the description to the left and right is the more accurate and is the one recorded here.

The three pointings are the best differentiators for this date and denomination. Counting the border beads is again not recommended.

Figure 17 – 1914 Threepence Obverses (1)

Obverse 2	Obverse 3
'I' points to right of bead	'I' points to left of bead

Figure 18 – 1914 Threepence Obverses (2)

Obverse 2	Obverse 3
'P' points to a bead	'P' points to a space

33

Figure 19 – 1914 Threepence Obverses (3)

Obverse 2
'D' points to a space

Obverse 3
'D' points to a bead

Minor Varieties:

There are no reported minor varieties for this date.

1919 Threepence:

Major Varieties:

There are no reported major varieties for this date.

Minor Varieties:

For 1919, there is a rare type where the last '9' in the date on the reverse is over an '8.' The normal coin is catalogued by Davies as no. 1932 whilst the overdate is no. 1933.

Figure 20 – 1919 Threepence Reverse

'9' over an '8'

There is also a minor variety where the second '9' in the date is narrower, more elongated and, therefore, taller, with the base of the tail of the '9' below the base line of the '1'. This type, which is not mentioned by Davies, also has a narrower gap between the '1' and the '9', when compared to the standard type.

Figure 21 – 1919 Threepence Reverse

Standard '9'	Elongated '9'
Base of '1' and '9' in line	'9' below the base of the '1'
Wide gap '1' to '9'	Narrower gap '1' to '9'

1920 Threepence:

Major Varieties:

There are no reported design varieties for the 1920 silver threepence. However, during this year, the Royal Mint debased the silver coinage of the UK from 92.5% to 50% silver. Either 40% copper and 10% nickel or 45% copper and 5% manganese were used as the additional metals to the alloy. This occurred during the production of the threepence and so there are examples of both alloy types found for this year. Differentiating them can be difficult as there are few easily distinguished signs to go by, especially on worn specimens. It is easy to verify which is which chemically, but attacking their coins with potentially damaging chemicals is hardly something the collector would want to do.

One way to distinguish them is to listen to the 'ring' they make when spun on a metal surface and allowed to come to rest. Sterling silver coins will give a low note, whilst for the debased silver it is higher. If in doubt, check the sound against an earlier date for sterling silver and a later one for debased silver.

A second way, which is only really viable for high quality specimens is to examine the serifs of the 'E's. Sterling silver coins have 'E's which are slightly sharper, due to the flow properties of the alloy used. A good magnifying glass is needed for this test and high grade specimens of both types in order to be able to see the differences.

Minor Varieties:

There are no reported minor varieties for this date.

1921 Threepence:

Major Varieties:

There are no reported major varieties for this date.

Minor Varieties:

There are no minor variations to the obverse for this date. However, the 1921 threepence has two minor reverse varieties based on the size of the '2' in the date, which can be either wide or narrow, and catalogued by Davies as numbers. 1936 and 1937 respectively. The difference in width is easy to see when a specimen of each is available for examination, but is more difficult in isolation. In the photographs below, the original size of each is 350 pixels squared and the difference in width of the '2' is just 10 pixels.

Figure 22 – 1921 Threepence Reverses

Wide '2'   Narrow '2'

1922 Threepence:

Major Varieties:

There are no reported major varieties for this date.

Minor Varieties:

There are no design variations for this date for either the obverse or reverse. However, the overall finish can be either dull or bright, the bright finish being the scarcer type. This arose from a change in the content of the alloy from 40% copper/10% nickel or 45% copper/5% Manganese to 50% copper, giving what is described as a blanched finish. Davies catalogues the dull finish as no. 1938 and the bright as no. 1939.

1926 Threepence:

Major Varieties:

Like the penny, this date has one of the most well known varieties of the 20th century series. There are two major obverse types, the earlier ordinary type (obverse 3) and the well known 'Modified Effigy' (obverse 4), each matched to a single reverse (reverse B), giving the two varieties for this date: 3+B and 4+B. Both types are catalogued by Davies with the numbers 1942 and 1943. The key identifier is the position of the initials 'BM' on the truncation.

Obverses:

Obverse 3: Obverse 3 is similar to the earlier obverses between 1914 and 1925 and can be identified by:

- The initials 'BM' on the truncation are towards the centre of the neck, and have two dots after them.
- The King has straight eyelids.
- The eye has no pupil.
- The under side to the nose is horizontal.
- The 'crow's' foot at the corner of the eye is poorly formed.
- The 'I' of 'GEORGIVS' points to a bead. Some cataloguers regard it as to the left of a bead.
- The border beads are rounded.
- The 'B' of 'BRITT' points to a border bead.
- The hair and the beard are less well defined.

Obverse 4: This is the well-known 'Modified Effigy' or 'ME' type, distinguished by:

- The most famous identifier is the position of the initials of Sir Bertram Mackennal (BM) on the neck truncation. These are found much further back on the neck and are without dots.
- The King's eyelids curve down.
- The eye has a distinct pupil.
- The underside of the nose curves slightly.
- The 'crow's' foot at the corner of the eye is symmetric.
- The 'I' of 'GEORGIVS' points to a space between beads.
- The border beads are elongated.
- The 'B' of 'BRITT' points to a space.
- The hair and the beard are less well defined.

Figure 23 – 1926 Threepence Obverses (1)

Obverse 3	**Obverse 4**
Ordinary Effigy	Modified Effigy
'BM' near centre	'BM' to the rear
'BM' has dots	'BM' has no dots

37

Figure 24 – 1926 Threepence Obverses (2)

Obverse 3	**Obverse 4**
Ordinary Effigy	Modified Effigy
Straight Eyelid	Curved Eyelid
Plain Eyeball	Eyeball with Pupil
Straight Underside to Nose	Curved Underside to Nose
Poor crow's foot	Distinct crow's foot

Figure 25 – 1926 Threepence Obverses (3)

Obverse 3	**Obverse 4**
'I' of 'GEORGIVS' to a bead	'I of 'GEORGIVS' to a space
Round border beads	Elongated border beads

Figure 26 – 1926 Threepence Obverses (4)

Obverse 3	**Obverse 4**
'B' of 'BRITT' to bead	'B' of 'BRITT' to space

The sharpness of the hair and beard is only really a useful identifier on high grade specimens. The indicators in the photographs above are a much better and more definitive means of differentiating the two types.

Minor Varieties:

There are no reported minor varieties for this date.

*   *   *   *   *

Denomination: Sixpence

1911 – 1927 (including the modified effigy)

1927 (proof) – 1936

Specification: Diameter: 19mm
Weight: 3.0g
Metal: Silver (92.5%) 1911 to 1920
              (50%) 1920 to 1936

Obverse Design:

George's bust facing left with abbreviated legend as follows:

1. 'GEORGIVS V DEI GRA: BRITT: OMN: REX' – 1911 to 1927
2. 'GEORGIVS V D. G. BRITT: OMN: REX F.D. IND: IMP:' – 1927 to 1936

Reverse Design:

1. A lion on a crown, separating the date and within an inner circle. Around the edge between the circle and the rim the words: 'FID: DEF: IND: IMP:' to the top and 'SIXPENCE' to the bottom – 1911 to 1927.

2. Six oak sprigs each with an acorn attached. Design has 'KG' at the centre and the words 'SIX PEN CE' and 'A date D' spaced equally round the coin – 1927 to 1936.

Edge: Milled

Years Produced: 1911 to 1936, except 1924 and 1929, for the business strike, plus specimens in the proof sets of 1911 and 1927.

Varieties:

Major varieties are found for the years 1911, 1920, 1925 and 1926, with minor varieties in 1911, 1919, 1922 and 1935. In 1927, there was a major design change with the 'acorn' reverse replacing the traditional crowned lion. However, the lion was used only on the currency coins of 1927, whilst the acorn appeared only on the proof coins in the sets for that year. Thus there are no varieties specified for 1927.

1911 Business Strike Sixpence:

Major Varieties:

There are four major varieties of the 1911 sixpence which has two obverses (obverses 1 and 2) and two reverses (reverses A and B), giving the die pairings 1+A, 1+B, 2+A, and 2+B. Davies describes all four types, designated with numbers 1860, 1861, 1862 and 1863 respectively, whilst other sources rarely differentiate them.

Obverses:

Obverse 1: There are several very obvious identifiers for this obverse:

- The 'I' of 'BRITT' points to a border bead.
- The king's head is 'hollow'. This is the well known hollow neck variety.
- The 'I' of 'DEI' points slightly to the left of a bead.
- The neck truncation ends in line with the space between the 'E' and 'X' of 'REX'.

Obverse 2: This type is identified by:

- The 'I' of 'BRITT' points between two border beads.
- The king's head is 'flat'. This is the so-called flat neck type.
- The 'I' of 'DEI' points slightly to the right of a border bead.
- The neck truncation ends in line with the centre of the base of the 'E' of 'REX'.

Figure 27 – 1911 Sixpence Obverses (1)

Obverse 1
'I' of 'BRITT' to bead

Obverse 2
'I' of 'BRITT' to space

Figure 28 – 1911 Sixpence Obverses (2)

Obverse 1
'I' of 'DEI' slightly
to left of a bead

Obverse 2
'I' of 'DEI' slightly
to right of a bead

Some sources describe the pointing of the 'I' in 'DEI' for obverse 1 as being to a space. However, this definitively is not the case. At best it is slightly to the left of a bead and that of obverse 2 is slightly to the right.

Figure 29 – 1911 Sixpence Obverses (3)

Obverse 1	**Obverse 2**
Truncation in line	Truncation in line
with gap	with the 'E'

The hollow neck and ordinary neck types are illustrated in figure 15 for the 1911 threepence.

Reverses:

Reverse A: There are several minor differentiators for this type:

- The colon after 'FID' points to a bead.
- The 'I' of 'FID' points to a space.
- The lion has a small face.
- The lion's ears are narrower but deeper.
- The lion's mane is larger.

Reverse B:

- The colon after 'FID' points to a space between beads.
- The 'I' of 'FID' points to a bead.
- The lion has a broader face.
- The lion's ears are wider but thinner.
- The lion has less mane hair.

Figure 30 – 1911 Sixpence Reverses (1)

Reverse A	**Reverse B**
Colon points to a bead	Colon points to a space
'I' of 'FID' to a space	'I' of 'FID' to a bead

Figure 31 – 1911 Sixpence Reverses (2)

<table>
<tr><td align="center">**Reverse A**
Smaller Face
The ears are smaller
The lion's mane is larger</td><td align="center">**Reverse B**
Broader face
The ears are larger
The lion's mane is smaller</td></tr>
</table>

Minor Varieties:

In addition to the major varieties, reverse A is also found as one of two sub-types, both of which are paired to obverse 2 only.

Minor Variety 2+A Type 1:

- An extra curl at the bottom of the lion's mane.
- A larger ear.

Minor Variety 2+A Type 2:

- No extra curl at the bottom of the lion's mane.
- A smaller ear.

The 2+A type 1 is the slightly scarcer of what is a scarce die type anyway. These minor types are not described by Davies.

Figure 32 – 1911 Sixpence Reverses (3)

<table>
<tr><td align="center">**Reverse A1**
Extra Curls
Ear is larger in height</td><td align="center">**Reverse A2**
No extra curls
Ear is lower in height</td></tr>
</table>

The ear of type A2 is very similar to that of reverse B, albeit slightly less wide, suggesting that it is perhaps an intermediate between reverse A1 and reverse B.

1919 Sixpence:

Major Varieties:

There are no reported major varieties for this date.

Minor Varieties:

There are two minor varieties for the 1919 sixpence, based on the size of the reverse inscription and the thickness of the rim.

Reverse B Type 1: This type is similar to the other coins from 1911 to 1925.

- Large lettering all round the design.
- A thin rim.
- Lettering is close to the rim beads.
- The letters are closer to the inner circle.

Reverse B Type 2:

- Smaller lettering all round the design.
- A thicker rim.
- Lettering is away from the rim beads.
- The letters are away from the inner circle.

These varieties are not mentioned in Davies.

Figure 33 – 1919 Sixpence Reverses

Reverse B1
Larger Letters
Thin rim
Letters close to the beads
Letters close to circle

Reverse B2
Smaller letters
Thicker rim
Letters away from beads
Letters away from circle

1920 Sixpence:

Major Varieties:

Like the threepence, there are no reported design varieties for the 1920 sixpence. During this year, the Royal Mint debased the silver coinage of the UK from 92.5% to 50% silver, and this occurred during the production of the sixpence leading to examples of both alloy types for this year. Davies catalogues the sterling silver type as no. 1872 whilst the debased type is 1873.

Differentiating them can be difficult as there are no easily distinguished signs to go by, especially on worn specimens. It is easy to verify which is which chemically, but this approach is not one recommended to collectors, as it involves the use of potentially damaging chemicals. One way to distinguish them is to listen to the 'ring' they make when spun on a metal surface and allowed to come to rest. Alternatively, they can be placed on a finger tip and struck gently with a pencil. Sterling silver coins will give a low note, whilst the debased silver is higher. If in doubt, the sound can be checked against an earlier date for sterling silver and a later one for debased silver.

Another way, which is available for high quality specimens, is to examine the serifs of the 'E's. Sterling silver coins have 'E's which are slightly sharper, due to the flow properties of the alloy used. A good magnifying glass is needed for this test and high grade specimens of both types in order to be able to see the differences.

Minor Varieties:

There are no reported minor varieties for this date.

1922 Sixpence:

Major Varieties:

There are no reported major varieties for this date.

Minor Varieties:

Again, as for the threepence, there are no design variations for this date for either the obverse or reverse. However, the overall finish can be either dull or bright, depending on the precise alloy mixture used, the bright finish being the scarcer type.

1925 Sixpence:

Major Varieties:

During 1925, the Royal Mint made design changes to both the obverse and reverse of the sixpence, but unusually, the resulting die pairs seem to have been changed at the same time. Thus there are two obverses, designated obverse 2 and obverse 3 and two reverses designated reverse B and reverse C. The result of the coincident pairing is that there are just two varieties: 2+B and 3+C. These are catalogued by Davies as numbers 1879 and 1880.

Obverses:

Obverse 2:

- The 'I' of 'DEI' points to a border bead.
- Coins have a narrow or thin rim.
- There are 146 border beads.

Obverse 3:

- The 'I' of 'DEI' points to a space between beads.
- Coins have a wide or broad rim.
- There are 128 elongated border teeth.

Figure 34 – 1925 Sixpence Obverses

Obverse 2	**Obverse C**
Narrow rim	Wide rim
'I' of 'DEI' points to bead	'I' of 'DEI' points to a space
Round border beads	Elongated border teeth

Reverses:

Reverse B:

- The colon after 'FID' points between two beads.
- Has a narrow or thin rim.
- The 'I' of IND' points to a space.
- Small border beads.

Reverse C:

- The colon after 'FID' points to the left of a bead.
- Has a wide or broad rim.
- The 'I' of 'IND' points to a bead.
- Fewer border beads than reverse B.
- Larger border beads.

Figure 35 – 1925 Sixpence Reverses (1)

Reverse B
Colon after 'FID'
points to a space
Smaller beads

Reverse C
Colon after 'FID'
points left of bead
Larger beads

Figure 36 – 1925 Sixpence Reverses (2)

Reverse B
Narrow rim
'I' of 'IND' points to space

Reverse C
Wide rim
'I' of 'IND' points to a bead

Minor Varieties:

There are no reported minor varieties for this date.

1926 Sixpence:

Major Varieties:

For many denominations 1926 was the year of the Modified Effigy, and the sixpence is no exception. There are two major obverse types, the earlier ordinary type (obverse 3) and the well known 'Modified Effigy' (obverse 4) each matched to a single reverse (reverse C). This gives the two varieties for this date: 3+C and 4+C. Both types are catalogued by Davies, with the numbers 1881 and 1882 respectively. The key identifier is the position of the initials 'BM' on the truncation.

Obverses:

Obverse 3: Obverse 3 is similar to the earlier obverses between 1921 and 1925 and can be identified by:

- The 'I' of 'DEI' points to a space.
- The initials 'BM' on the truncation are towards the centre of the neck, and have two dots after them.

46

- The King has straight eyelids.
- The eye has no pupil.
- A horizontal under side to the nose.
- A broader rim.
- 128 border beads.
- The 'I' of 'GEORGIVS' points to a bead/left of a bead.
- The border beads are rounded.
- The 'B' of 'BRITT' points to a border bead.

Obverse 4: This is the well-known 'Modified Effigy' or 'ME' type:

- The 'I' of 'DEI' points to a bead.
- The most famous identifier: the position of the initials of Sir Bertram Mackennal (BM) on the neck truncation. These are found much further back on the neck and are without dots.
- The King's eyelids curve down.
- The eye has a distinct pupil.
- The underside of the nose curves slightly.
- A narrower rim, but not as narrow as the pre-1925 obverse 2 rim.
- 127 border beads.
- The 'I' of 'GEORGIVS' points to a space between beads.
- The border beads are elongated.
- The 'B' of 'BRITT' points to a space.

Figure 37 – 1926 Sixpence Obverses

Obverse 3
Wide rim
'I' of 'DEI' points to space

Obverse 4
Narrower rim
'I' of 'DEI' points to a bead

All the other identifiers for the obverses of the ordinary and modified effigy sixpences are identical to those for the threepence of the same date. Illustrations can be seen in figures 23-26 and are not repeated here.

Minor Varieties:

There are no reported minor varieties for this date.

1935 Sixpence:

Major Varieties:

There are no reported major varieties for this date.

Minor Varieties:

Davies mentions, but does not catalogue, that the 1935 sixpence is found as one of two minor varieties, based on small differences in the reverse design (Reverse F), and numbered 1899 and 1900.

Reverse F Type 1: This is the much rarer variety and can be identified by:

- Smaller border beads.
- Thinner stems to the acorns.
- The legend being further away from the beads.

Reverse F Type 2:

- Larger border beads.
- Thicker stems to the acorns.
- The legend being closer to the beads.

*   *   *   *   *

Denomination: Shilling

1911 – 1927 (including the modified effigy)

1927 - 1936

Specification: Diameter: 24mm
Weight: 5.7g
Metal: Silver (92.5%) 1911 to 1919
(50%) 1920 to 1936

Obverse Design:

George's bust facing left with abbreviated legend as follows:

'GEORGIVS V DEI GRA: BRITT: OMN: REX' – 1911 to 1936

Reverse Design:

1. For the first design up to 1927, a lion on a crown, separating the date and within an inner circle. Around the edge between the circle and the rim the words: 'FID: DEF: IND: IMP:' to the top and 'ONE SHILLING' to the bottom.

2. For the second reverse, a different design of lion on a crown and no circle, with the words 'FID · DEF' around the top left, 'IND · IMP' around the top right. The words 'ONE · SHILLING · 19XX' around the bottom of the reverse.

Edge: Milled

Years Produced: 1911 to 1936, plus proofs in the sets of 1911 and 1927.

Varieties:

Major varieties of the business strikes are found for the years 1911, 1912, 1920, 1921, 1926 and 1927, with minor varieties in 1920, 1921, and 1925 only. For the proof coins, there are both major and minor varieties for the 1911 strike.

49

1911 Business Strike Shilling:

Major Varieties:

There are three major varieties of the 1911 shilling based on three obverses (obverses 1, 2 and 3) and a single reverse (reverse A), giving the die pairings 1+A, 2+A, and 3+A. Davies describes all three types, with the numbers 1790, 1791 and 1792 respectively, whilst other sources rarely differentiate them. All three are about equally scarce.

Obverses:

Obverse 1: There are several identifiers for this obverse:

- Hollow neck.
- The 'I' of 'GEORGIVS' points to a space between beads.
- 172 border beads.
- The 'D' of 'DEI' points to a space between beads.

Obverse 2: This type is identified by:

- Hollow neck.
- The 'I' of 'GEORGIVS' points to a bead.
- 173 border beads.
- The 'D' of 'DEI' points to a bead.

Obverse 3: This type is identified by:

- Flat neck.
- The 'I' of 'GEORGIVS' points to a bead.
- 173 border beads.
- The 'D' of 'DEI' points to a bead.

Of these identifiers, counting border beads is not recommended as the first choice option for determining which coin is which.

Figure 38 – 1911 Shilling Obverses (1)

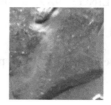

Obverses 1 & 2
Hollow Neck

Obverse 3
Flat Neck

Figure 39 – 1911 Shilling Obverses (2)

Obverse 1
'I' of 'GEORGIVS' to space

Obverses 2 & 3
'I' of 'GEORGIVS' to bead

Figure 40 – 1911 Shilling Obverses (3)

Obverse 1
'D' of 'DEI' to space

Obverses 2 & 3
'D' of 'DEI' to bead

Minor Varieties:

There are no reported minor varieties for the 1911 business strike shilling.

1911 Proof Strike Shilling:

Major Varieties:

According to Davies, there are unconfirmed reports of proof versions of two of the business strike shilling varieties i.e. 1+A, 2+A, with the 3+A variety being the 'normal' proof striking. The photographs in figures 38 – 40 illustrate the identifiers and are not repeated here.

Minor Varieties:

Davies also reports that the 3+A proof exists as one of two minor types, based on the shape of the rim and catalogued with numbers 1792 and 1793. One type has the normal square rim edge and the other has the edge chamfered. Both seem to be about equally common.

51

1912 Shilling:

Major Varieties:

There are two major varieties of the 1912 shilling. In this case, there is a single obverse (obverse 3) and two reverses (reverses A and B), giving the die pairings 3+A and 3+B. These are catalogued by Davies with numbers 1794 and 1795 respectively.

Reverses:

Reverse A:

- Smaller letters in the legend.
- The letters of 'IMP' are closer together.
- The letters of 'IMP' and following colon are spread over 14 border beads.
- The upright of the 'P' in 'IMP' points to a border bead.
- There are 178 border beads.

Reverse B:

- Larger letters in the legend.
- The letters of 'IMP' are more widespread, especially the 'M' and 'P'.
- The letters of 'IMP' and following colon are spread over 16 border beads.
- The upright of the 'P' in 'IMP' points to a space between border beads.
- There are 180 border beads.

As for other denominations, counting border beads is not recommended as the best identifier for the two types.

Figure 41 – 1912 Shilling Reverses

Reverse A	**Reverse B**
Smaller letters	Larger lettering
Narrow spacing of 'IMP'	Wider spacing of 'IMP'
'P' points to a bead	'P' points to a space

Minor Varieties:

There are no reported minor varieties for the 1912 shilling.

1920 Shilling:

There are two major varieties of the 1920 shilling which are based on two obverses (obverses 3 and 4) and a single reverse (reverse B), giving the die pairings 3+B and 4+B. Interestingly, and unlike other coins of this date, the shilling is only found in 50% silver with no examples struck in sterling (92.5%) silver. Davies catalogues the two types as numbers 1803 and 1804.

Major Varieties:

Obverses:

Obverse 3: There are several identifiers for this obverse:

- The 'I' of 'GEORGIVS' points to a border bead.
- Wider rim.
- High relief and small effigy.
- Flat neck.
- The colon after 'OMN' points to a space between beads.
- 173 border beads.
- The colon after 'GRA' points to the left of a border bead.
- The colon after 'BRITT' points to the right of a bead, described by some as to a space between beads.

Obverse 4: This type is identified by:

- The 'I' of 'GEORGIVS' points to a space between border beads.
- Narrower rim.
- Low relief and larger effigy.
- Signs of a hollow neck.
- The colon after 'OMN' points to a bead.
- 174 border beads.
- The colon after 'GRA' points to the left of a space between border beads.
- The colon after 'BRITT' points to a bead.

Figure 42 – 1920 Shilling Obverses (1)

Obverse 3	Obverse 4
Wider rim	Narrower rim
'I' points to a bead	'I' points to a space

53

Figure 43 – 1920 Shilling Obverses (2)

Obverse 3
High relief effigy
Smaller bust

Obverse 4
Low relief effigy
Larger bust

Figure 44 – 1920 Shilling Obverses (3)

 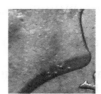

Obverse 3
Flat Neck

Obverse 4
Slight hollowing of neck

Figure 45 – 1920 Shilling Obverses (4)

Obverse 3
Colon of 'OMN' to a space

Obverse 4
Colon of 'OMN' to a bead

Figure 46 – 1920 Shilling Obverses (5)

Obverse 3
Colon after 'GRA'
to left of bead

Obverse 4
Colon after 'GRA'
to left of space

Figure 47 – 1920 Shilling Obverses (6)

Obverse 3	**Obverse 4**
Colon after 'BRITT'	Colon after 'BRITT'
to right of bead	to a bead

Minor Varieties:

Although obverse 3 of the 1920 shilling is usually found with the thicker rim, there are examples with thinner milling to the edge.

There are also examples of both obverse 3 and obverse 4 having a blanched surface giving a bright finish.

1921 Shilling:

Major Varieties:

There are five major types of 1921 shilling. There are three obverses (obverse 3, obverse 4 and obverse 5) and two reverses (reverses D and E), giving the die pairings 3+D, 4+D, 4+E, 5+D and 5+E. There are no reports of the die pairing 3+E being found.

Obverses:

Obverse 3:

- The 'I' of 'GEORGIVS' points to a border bead.
- High relief, small effigy, as per 1920 and earlier.
- Flat neck.
- Wider rim.
- The colon after 'OMN' points to a space between beads.
- The colon after 'BRITT' points to the right of a bead, described by some as to a space between beads.
- 173 border beads.
- The colon after 'GRA' points to the left of a border bead.

Obverse 4:

- The 'I' of 'GEORGIVS' points to a space between border beads.
- Low relief, larger effigy.

55

- Signs of a hollow neck.
- Narrower rim.
- The colon after 'OMN' points to a bead.
- The colon after 'BRITT' points to a bead.
- 174 border beads.
- The colon after 'GRA' points to the right of a border bead.

Obverse 5:

- The 'I' of 'GEORGIVS' points to a border bead.
- Low relief, larger effigy.
- Signs of a hollow neck.
- Narrower rim.
- The colon after 'OMN' points to a bead.
- The colon after 'BRITT' points to a space between beads.
- 178 border beads.
- The colon after 'GRA' points to the right of a border bead.

Figure 48 – 1921 Shilling Obverses (1)

Obverse 3	**Obverse 4**	**Obverse 5**
'I' points to a bead	'I' points to a space	'I' points to a bead.

Figure 49 – 1921 Shilling Obverses (2)

Obverse 3	**Obverses 4 & 5**
High relief effigy	Low relief effigy
Smaller bust	Larger bust
Flat neck	Signs of a hollow neck.

Figure 50 – 1921 Shilling Obverses (3)

Obverse 3	**Obverse 4**	**Obverse 5**
Colon of 'OMN' to space	Colon of 'OMN' to bead	Colon of 'OMN' to bead
Wider rim	Narrower rim	Narrower rim

Figure 51 – 1921 Shilling Obverses (4)

Obverse 3	**Obverse 4**	**Obverse 5**
Colon of 'BRITT'	Colon of 'BRITT'	Colon of 'BRITT'
right of a bead	to a bead	to a space

Figure 52 – 1921 Shilling Obverses (5)

Obverse 3	**Obverse 4**	**Obverse 5**
Colon of 'GRA'	Colon of 'GRA'	Colon of 'GRA'
left of a bead	to right of bead	to right of bead

Reverses:

Reverse D:

- The tuft of the lion's tail is between the 'I' and the 'M'.
- The tuft appears higher up the field, sometimes described as bracketing the 'I' of 'IMP'.
- The right leg of the 'N' in 'IND' points to a bead, described by some, and correctly so, as being to the right of a bead.
- The 'I' of 'FID' points to the left of a bead.
- The 'P' of 'IMP' points to the right of a bead.

Reverse E:

- The tuft of the lion's tail is closer to the 'M'.
- The tuft appears lower in the field and points to the 'I' and the 'M' of 'IMP'.
- The right leg of the 'N' in 'IND' points to a space between beads, regarded by some, and again correctly so, as being to the left of a border bead.
- The 'I' of 'FID' points to the right side of a space between border beads.
- The 'P' of 'IMP' points to the right side of a space.

Figure 53 – 1921 Shilling Reverses (1)

Reverse D	**Reverse E**
Tuft between 'I' and 'M'	Tuft close to the 'M'
Tail higher in the field	Tail lower in the field

Figure 54 – 1921 Shilling Reverses (2)

Reverse D	**Reverse E**
Right leg of 'N' in	Right leg of 'N' in
'IND' to right of bead	'IND' to left of bead

Figure 55 – 1921 Shilling Reverses (3)

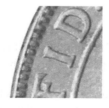

Reverse D	**Reverse E**
'I' in 'FID'	'I' in 'FID'
to left of a bead	to right of a space

58

Figure 56 – 1921 Shilling Reverses (4)

Reverse D
'P' in 'IMP'
to right of bead

Reverse E
'P' of 'IMP'
to right of space

Minor Varieties:

1. There are also examples of the die pairs 3+D, 4+D, 5+D and 5+E having a blanched surface giving a bright finish. This was caused by the use of manganese in place of nickel in the alloy. These varieties are scarce.

2. The die pair 3+D has also been found on examples with a thinner flan, but is very rare.

3. There is also a minor variety of the die pair 3+D on which the reverse design is smaller and the base strokes of the 'E' in 'ONE' and the first 'L' in 'SHILLING' are thinner.

Variety 3+D Type 1:

- Normal sized reverse design.
- The base stroke to the first 'L' in 'SHILLING' is thicker.
- The base line of the 'E' in 'ONE' is thicker.
- The edge is a normal size and shape.

Variety 3+D Type 2: This minor type is rare compared to the standard coin.

- Smaller sized reverse design.
- The base stroke to the first 'L' in 'SHILLING' is thinner.
- The base line of the 'E' in 'ONE' is thinner.
- The edge is a normal size and shape.

Figure 57 – 1921 Shilling Reverses (5)

Reverse D1
Thicker base line to first 'L'

Reverse D2
Thinner base line to first 'L'

59

Figure 58 – 1921 Shilling Reverses (6)

Reverse D1
Thicker base line to 'E'
Normal edge

Reverse D2
Thinner base line to 'E'
Rolled edge

1922 Shilling:

Major Varieties:

There are no major varieties for the 1922 shilling.

Minor Varieties:

All coins described for this year have obverse 5 paired with reverse E. However, there are two minor varieties of this pairing, one with the normal reverse and the other with a slightly larger design, defined by Davies as 22mm. They are numbered 1810 and 1811 respectively by Davies. It is not easy to differentiate the two types unless they are placed side by side when the size difference is subtle but obvious. However, two key features do distinguish them.

Reverse E Type 1:

- The lion's body is thin measured from back to chest.
- The width of the large tuft at the end of the tail is thinner.

Reverse E Type 2:

- The lion's body is thicker from back to chest.
- The width of the large tuft at the end of the tail is wider.

Figure 59– 1922 Shilling Reverses

Normal Reverse E1
Thinner body
Thinner tuft

Larger Reverse E2
Thicker body
Wider tuft

The normal design is also found with either a dull finish or a bright one, due to changes in the metal content of the alloy of silver used. There are also reports of the larger reverse design type being found with a bright finish, meaning that there are potentially four minor varieties for this date. Davies catalogues these latter bright finish types with numbers 1812 and 1813.

1925 Shilling:

Major Varieties:

There are no major varieties for the 1925 shilling.

Minor Varieties:

There are two minor varieties of this denomination and date. Neither is particularly rare. Like the 1911 proof striking, there are 1925 shillings with a normal edge and others with a chamfered rim. These are specified by Davies and numbered 1817 and 1818.

1926 Shilling:

Major Varieties:

Like other denominations, the 1926 shilling has two obverse types (obverses 5 and 6) which are paired with a single reverse (reverse F) giving the die pairs 5+F and 6+F. Obverse 5 is the obverse found on shillings between 1921 and 1925, whilst obverse 6 is the well known 'Modified Effigy' type.

Obverses:

Obverse 5: This obverse can be identified by:

- The 'I' of 'DEI' points to a space.
- Narrower rim than the 'ME' obverse.
- The border beads are small and rounded, with wide gap to legend.
- The initials 'BM' on the truncation are towards the centre of the neck, and have two dots after them.
- The King has straight eyelids.
- The eye has no distinct pupil.
- The 'crow's foot' at the corner of the eye is poorly defined.
- Horizontal under side to the nose.
- 178 border beads.
- The 'I' of 'GEORGIVS' points to a bead.
- The 'B' of 'BRITT' points to a space between border beads.
- The tip of the truncation is sharp.
- The hair and the beard are less well defined.

Obverse 6: This is the well-known 'Modified Effigy' type, distinguished by:

- The 'I' of 'DEI' points to a bead.
- Slightly wider rim.
- The border beads are larger and elongated, with narrower gap to legend.
- The most famous identifier: the position of the initials of Sir Bertram Mackennal (BM) on the neck truncation. These are found much further back on the neck and are without dots.
- The King's eyelids curve down.
- The eye has a distinct pupil.
- The 'crow's foot' at the corner of the eye is better defined.
- The underside of the nose curves slightly.
- 136 border beads.
- The 'I' of 'GEORGIVS' points to a space between beads.
- The 'B' of 'BRITT' points to a bead.
- The tip of the truncation is blunt.
- The hair and beard are more finely lined.

Although the identifiers are broadly the same as for the lower denominations, one or two are different.

Figure 60 – 1926 Shilling Obverses (1)

Obverse 5	Obverse 6
Thin rim	Wider rim
'I' of 'DEI' points to space	'I' of 'DEI' points to a bead
Border beads small and round	Border beads are elongated
Wide gap, beads to legend	Small gap, beads to legend

Figure 61 – 1926 Shilling Obverses (2)

Obverse 5	Obverse 6
Ordinary Effigy	Modified Effigy
'BM' near centre	'BM' to the rear
'BM' has dots	'BM' has no dots

62

Figure 62 – 1926 Shilling Obverses (3)

Obverse 5	**Obverse 6**
Ordinary Effigy	Modified Effigy
Straight Eyelid	Curved Eyelid
No Eyeball	Eyeball
Straight Underside to Nose	Curved Underside to Nose
Poorly defined 'crow's foot'	Better defined 'crow's foot'

Figure 63 – 1926 Shilling Obverses (4)

Obverse 5
'I' of 'GEORGIVS' to bead

Obverse 6
'I' of 'GEORGIVS' to space

Figure 64 – 1926 Shilling Obverses (5)

Obverse 5
'B' of 'BRITT' to a space

Obverse 6
'B' of 'BRITT' to a bead

Figure 65 – 1926 Shilling Obverses (6)

Obverse 5
Sharply pointed truncation

Obverse 6
Bluntly pointed truncation

The sharpness of the hair and beard are only apparent on high grade examples and are not recommended as definitive identifiers, nor is counting border beads.

Minor Varieties:

There are no minor varieties for the 1926 shilling.

1927 Business Strike Shilling:

Major Varieties:

In 1927, the Royal Mint struck shillings with the same obverse and reverse as for 1926 i.e. with obverse 6 and reverse F. However they also introduced new reverse designs for the silver coinage, and issued all the new coins in a 6-coin proof set. All the other denominations for that year were produced for the proof set only, but the shilling was produced with the new reverse as a business strike as well.

Care is needed when assessing the coins in a 1927 set, in case a business strike shilling has been introduced into the set. This is particularly important where sets have been reconstituted. Thus there are two types of 1927 shilling. However, they can't be really regarded as varieties as they represent entirely different designs, with too many features to describe as differentiators. For this reason, I have simply included photographs of examples of each type here as the differences are obvious.

Figure 66 – 1927 Shilling Reverses

Old Reverse   New Reverse

Minor Varieties:

There are no minor varieties for the 1927 shilling.

*   *   *   *   *

Denomination: Florin

1911 – 1926

1927 (Proof) - 1936

Specification: Diameter: 28.5mm
Weight: 11.3g
Metal: Silver (92.5%) 1911 to 1919
(50%) 1920 to 1936

Obverse Design:

George's bust facing left with abbreviated legend as follows:

1. 'GEORGIVS V D. G. BRITT: OMN: REX F.D.IND: IMP:' – 1911 to 1926
2. 'GEORGIVS V DEI GRA: BRITT: OMN: REX' – 1927 to 1936

Reverse Design:

1. For the first design up to 1926, four crowned cruciform shields with sceptres in the angles. Around the top of the coin, the inscription 'ONE FLORIN' and below, the date.

2. For the second reverse, from 1927 to 1936, a new design of the shields and sceptres, with the words: 'FID◆DEF IND◆IMP' around the top and the date followed by 'ONE FLORIN' around the bottom.

Edge: Milled

Years Produced: 1911 to 1936, except 1927 and 1934 for the business strike, plus proofs in the sets of 1911 and 1927.

65

Varieties:

Major varieties of the business strikes are found for the years 1911, 1914, 1920, and 1923, with minor varieties in 1913, 1914, 1918, 1920, 1922 and 1923. For the proof strikes, there is a major variety for the 1911 coin. Interestingly, for this denomination, there is no 'Modified Effigy' variety for 1926 and, unlike the shilling, the 1927 strike is found in the proof sets only.

1911 Business Strike Florin:

Major Varieties:

There are two major varieties of the 1911 florin based on two obverses (obverses 1 and 2) and a single reverse (reverse A), giving the die pairings 1+A and 2+A. These are catalogued as numbers 1730 and 1731 respectively by Davies. Of these, obverse 1 is slightly scarcer.

Obverses:

Obverse 1: There are several identifiers for this scarcer obverse:

- Hollow neck.
- The 'I' of 'GEORGIVS' points to the right of a bead.
- The 'D' of 'F.D.' points to the left of a bead.
- There are 172 small border beads.
- The 'I' of 'IND' points to the right of a border bead.

Obverse 2: This type is identified by:

- Flat neck.
- The 'I' of 'GEORGIVS' points to a space between beads.
- The 'D' of 'F.D.' points to a space between beads.
- There are 169 small border beads.
- The 'I' of 'IND' points to a bead.

Several publications, including Davies, describe obverse 1 as having the 'I' of 'GEORGIVS' to a bead, but examination of these coins shows that the pointing is actually to the right of a bead and almost to a space, making it quite a fine distinction from obverse 2.

These two obverses have also been described as having the 'D' of 'F.D.' to a bead or a space. Again, the pointing of the 'D' (for obverse 1) to a bead is more accurately described as to the left of a bead. Similarly, the pointing of the 'I' in 'IND' for obverse 1 is more accurately to the right of a bead, although sometimes described as to a space.

Even the hollow neck feature is not particularly pronounced and so for once, counting border beads is very much the defining characteristic for these two types.

Figure 67 – 1911 Florin Obverses (1)

Obverse 1
Hollow Neck

Obverse 2
Flat Neck

Figure 68 – 1911 Florin Obverses (2)

Obverse 1
'I' of 'GEORGIVS' to right of bead

Obverse 2
'I' of 'GEORGIVS' to space

Figure 69 – 1911 Florin Obverses (3)

Obverse 1
'D' of 'F.D.' to left of a bead

Obverse 2
'D' of 'F.D.' to space

Figure 70 – 1911 Florin Obverses (4)

Obverse 1
'I' of 'IND' to right of bead

Obverse 2
'I' of 'IND' to bead

Minor Varieties:

There are no reported minor varieties for the 1911 business strike florin.

1911 Proof Strike Florin:

Major Varieties:

As for the business strike, the proof strike florin for 1911 is found as two major types, based on two obverses (obverses 1 and 2) and a single reverse (reverse A), giving the die pairings 1+A and 2+A. Both are about equal scarce and have the same catalogue numbers as the business strike. The identifiers for these two types are exactly the same as for the business strike and are illustrated in figures 67 – 70.

1913 Florin:

Major Varieties:

There are no major design varieties for the 1913 florin, which is catalogued as having obverse 2, reverse C.

Minor Varieties:

There are two minor varieties of the 1913 florin based on small changes to the reverse design. These reverses are either the 'normal' reverse as found on the 1911 and 1912 florins or a scarcer type having a smaller design. Both types are catalogued as die pair 2+C with Davies catalogue numbers 1733 and 1734 respectively.

Reverse C Type 1 (Normal):

- The second '1' in the date points to the right of a border bead.
- There is a smaller gap between the second '1' in the date and the border beads.
- There is a wider gap between the second '1' in the date and the shield.
- There is a wider gap between the '9' in the date and the point of the shield.
- The gap between the date/inscription and the edge is smaller.
- The gap between the 'F' of 'FLORIN' and the point of the shield is wider.
- The gap between the 'N' of 'FLORIN' and the Scottish shield is slightly wider.

Reverse C Type 2 (Smaller):

- The second '1' in the date points to a space between border beads.
- There is a wider gap between the second '1' in the date and the border beads.
- There is a narrower gap between the second '1' in the date and the shield.
- There is a smaller gap between the '9' in the date and the point of the shield.
- The gap between the date/inscription and the edge is wider.
- The gap between the 'F' of 'FLORIN' and the point of the shield is smaller.
- The gap between the 'N' of 'FLORIN' and the Scottish shield is slightly smaller.

Figure 71 – 1913 Florin Reverses (1)

Normal Reverse C1
Second '1' to right of bead
Small gap '1' to bead
Wider gap '1' to shield

Smaller Reverse C2
Second '1' to a space
Wider gap '1' to bead
Narrower gap '1' to shield

Figure 72 – 1913 Florin Reverses (2)

Normal Reverse C1
Wider gap '9' to shield

Smaller Reverse C2
Narrower gap '9' to shield

Figure 73 – 1913 Florin Reverses (3)

Normal Reverse C1
Wider gap 'F' to shield
Wider gap 'N' to shield
Narrow gap letters to beads

Smaller Reverse C2
Narrow gap 'F' to shield
Narrow gap 'N' to shield
Wider gap letters to beads

The smaller design type is also found as one of two sub-varieties where the '13' of the date is either normal or widely spaced. This type is mentioned by Davies, but is not given a catalogue number.

Figure 74 – 1913 Florin Reverses (4)

Normal Narrow '13'   Wider spaced '13'

1914 Florin:

Major Varieties:

There is a single obverse for the 1914 florin (obverse 2) paired with three reverses (reverse C, reverse D and reverse E) giving the die pairs 2+C, 2+D and 2+E. None is especially rare, although the 2+C and 2+D are somewhat scarcer. Davies Catalogues these three types as numbers 1735, 1736 and 1737.

Reverses:

Reverse C:

- The top of the crown on the harp's shield points to a border bead.
- Has smaller border beads.
- Has a thin rim.
- The crosses on the crowns are away from the border beads.
- The 'N' of 'FLORIN' is nearer to the shield than the border beads.
- The words 'ONE FLORIN' and '1914' are further away from the design.
- The 'L' of 'FLORIN' points to a space between border beads.
- The top bar of the 'F' of 'FLORIN' is slightly misaligned with the 'L'.
- The lettering is large.

Reverse D:

- The top of the crown on the harp's shield points to a border bead.
- Has smaller border beads.
- Has a thicker rim.
- The crosses on the crowns are away from the border beads.
- The 'N' of 'FLORIN' is equidistant from the shield and the border beads.
- The words 'ONE FLORIN' and '1914' are furthest away from the design.
- The 'L' of 'FLORIN' points to a space between border beads.
- The top bar of the 'F' of 'FLORIN' is slightly misaligned with the 'L'.
- The lettering is large.

Reverse E:

- The top of the crown on the harp's shield points to a space between beads.
- Has larger border beads.
- Has a thicker rim.
- The crosses on the crowns are closer to the border beads.
- The 'N' of 'FLORIN' is close to the shield.
- The words 'ONE FLORIN' and '1914' are closer to the design.
- The 'L' of 'FLORIN' points to a border bead.
- The top bar of the 'F' of 'FLORIN' is now aligned wit the 'L'.
- The lettering is smaller.

Figure 75 – 1914 Florin Reverses (1)

Reverse C	**Reverse D**	**Reverse E**
Crown points to a bead	Crown points to a bead	Crown points to a space
Small Beads	Small Beads	Larger Beads
Thin Rim	Thicker Rim	Thicker Rim
Cross away from beads	Cross away from beads	Cross closer to beads

Figure 76 – 1914 Florin Reverses (2)

Reverse C	**Reverse D**	**Reverse E**
'N' closer to shield than edge	Gap 'N' to shield equal to gap to edge	'N' much closer to shield
Letters away from design	Letters far away from design	Letters closer to design

Figure 77 – 1914 Florin Reverses (3)

Reverse C	**Reverse D**	**Reverse E**
'L' to a space	'L' to a space	'L' to a bead
'F' is below the 'L'	F' is below the 'L'	'F aligned with 'L'

The size of the lettering is a very difficult indicator to use to distinguish the types and one of the clearer methods illustrated here should be used.

Minor Varieties:

The 1914 florin with reverse D is found as one of three minor varieties, the differences relating to the date and its pointings:

Reverse D Type 1: The upright of the '4' in the date points to a border bead.
Reverse D2 Type 2: The upright of the '4' points to a space giving a slightly narrower date.
Reverse D Type 3: The upright of the '4' points to the right of a bead, giving the widest spaced date.

Of these, the third is the common type for reverse D, the others being considerably scarcer.

Figure 78 – 1914 Florin Reverses (4)

Reverse D1	**Reverse D2**	**Reverse D3**
Leg of '4' to bead	Leg of '4' to space	Leg of '4' to right of bead
Normal space '1' to '4'	Narrow space '1' to '4'	Widest space '1' to '4'

1918 Florin:

Major Varieties:

There are no major design varieties for the 1918 florin, which is catalogued as having obverse 2, reverse E and is numbered 1741 by Davies.

Minor Varieties:

There are two minor varieties of the 1918 florin based on small changes to the reverse design. These reverses are either the 'normal' reverse as found on the 1914 to 1924 florins (except 1921) or a scarcer type having a smaller design. However, both types are catalogued as die pair 2+E by Davies, although they are separately catalogued with numbers 1741 and 1742 respectively.

Reverse E Type 1 (Normal):

- The gap between the end of the sceptre and the 'N' in 'ONE' is smaller.
- The gap between the end of the sceptre and the 'O' in 'FLORIN' is again small.
- The gap between the second '1' in the date and the shield is larger.

Reverse E Type 2 (Smaller):

- The gap between the end of the sceptre and the 'N' in 'ONE' is wider.
- The gap between the end of the sceptre and the 'O' in 'FLORIN' is larger.
- The gap between the second '1' in the date and the shield is smaller

Figure 79 – 1918 Florin Reverses (1)

| **Normal Reverse E1** | **Smaller Reverse E2** |
| Small gap sceptre to 'N' | Wider gap sceptre to 'N' |

Figure 80 – 1918 Florin Reverses (2)

| **Normal Reverse E1** | **Smaller Reverse E2** |
| Small gap sceptre to 'O' | Wider gap sceptre to 'O' |

Figure 81 – 1918 Florin Reverses (3)

Normal Reverse E1
Wider gap '1' to Shield

Smaller Reverse E2
Smaller gap '1' to Shield

The 'normal' reverse E1, Davies 1741, is found as one of two sub-varieties:

Reverse E Type 1 – 1: This is the common type, with a wider rim.
Reverse E Type 1 – 2: This rarer type has a narrower rim.

The smaller reverse E2, Davies 1742, is found as one of three sub-varieties. The differentiators revolve around the pointing of the second '1' in the date:

Reverse E Type 2 – 1: '1' pointing to a border bead and the centre line of the '8' pointing to a space between beads.
Reverse E Type 2 – 2: '1' pointing nearly to a space between border beads and the centre line of the '8' pointing to the left of a bead.
Reverse E Type 2 – 3: '1' pointing to the right of a border bead and the centre line of the '8' pointing to the left of a bead. This type also has very slightly smaller border beads than the other two types.

The third type described above can also be found with a double struck second '1' in the date.

1920 Florin:

Major Varieties:

There are two obverses for the 1920 florin (obverse 2 and obverse 3) paired with a single reverse (reverse E) giving the die pairs 2+E and 3+E. Davies classifies these with numbers 1744 and 1746. Neither is especially rare, although the 3+E type is scarcer. Unlike the smaller denominations for this date, there are no varieties based on metal content, as all were struck in 50% silver.

Obverses:

Obverse 2:

- The 'I of 'GEORGIVS' points to a space between border beads.
- The 'I' of 'BRITT' points to a border bead.
- It has a small high relief effigy.
- There are 169 border beads.
- The bust has a flat neck.

Obverse 3:

- The 'I of 'GEORGIVS' points to a border bead.
- The 'I' of 'BRITT' points between border beads.
- Larger low relief effigy.
- There are 175 border beads.
- The bust has signs of a hollow neck.

Figure 82 – 1920 Florin Obverses (1)

Obverse 2	**Obverse 3**
'I' of 'GEORGIVS' to space	'I' of 'GEORGIVS' to bead

Figure 83 – 1920 Florin Obverses (2)

Obverse 2	**Obverse 3**
'I' of 'BRITT' to a bead	'I' of 'BRITT' to a space

Figure 84 – 1920 Florin Obverses (3)

Obverse 2	**Obverse 3**
High Relief	Low Relief
Smaller bust	Larger bust
Flat neck	Slightly hollow neck

Minor Varieties;

Davies identifies a minor variety of the 1920 florin, classified as number 1745, where a smaller reverse design (reverse E) is paired with obverse 2. The normal size reverse is the more common of the two.

Variety 2+E Type 1 (Normal):

- More rounded, smaller beads at the top of the coin.
- Greater spacing between beads.

Variety 2+E Type 2 (Smaller):

- More elongated, larger beads at the top of the coin.
- Smaller spacing between beads.

There are a number of other minor differences between the two types, but these rely on very small measurements of the size of the design and the gaps between elements of it, which are very hard to appreciate with the naked eye.

Figure 85 – 1920 Florin Reverses (1)

Reverse E1 Normal	**Reverse E2 Small**
Small rounded beads	Larger elongated beads
Space between beads	Tiny gap between beads

Some sources quote the centring of the '0' in the date as a further differentiator for these two reverses, but this ignores the fact that there are rare varieties for the small reverse coin where the centring is the same as for the large design. However, it is true that the large design does have the '0' centred on a border bead whilst the more common of the small reverse designs has the '0' centred over a space between border beads. If any confusion arises, it may be settled by examining the border beads as described above.

Similarly, the spacing of the date is sometimes quoted as a defining character. Certainly, it is narrowest on the 'normal' reverse type, yet again it differs on the small reverse varieties, so it cannot be used with certainty.

The small reverse, 2+E2 type, 1920 florin consists of one of three sub-varieties:

Variety 2+E Type 2 Small - 1: The '0' is centred over a space. The spacing of the '20' is wider than on the 'normal' reverse. This is the most common of the small reverse types.
Variety 2+E Type 2 Small - 2: The '0' is centred over a border bead, with the same spacing as above.
Variety 2+E Type 2 Small - 3: The '0' is nearly centred over a bead and the date is the widest.

Figure 86 – 1920 Florin Reverses (2)

Reverse E1 Normal
Narrowly spaced '20'
'0' centred on a bead

Reverse E2 Small - 1
Intermediately spaced '20'
'0' centred on a space

Reverse E2 Small - 2
Intermediately spaced '20'
'0' centred on a bead

Reverse E2 Small - 3
Widely spaced '20'
'0' centred nearly on a bead

1922 Florin:

Major Varieties:

There are no major design varieties for the 1922 florin, which is catalogued as having obverse 3, reverse E.

Minor Varieties:

Specimens of the 1922 florin are found as one of two minor varieties. As for the smaller denominations, there were two types of finish produced, even though the silver content is the same for both. They can be either dull finish or bright finish, with the bright finish being somewhat scarcer, and can be difficult to differentiate except when in mint condition. Davies identifies the two types of finish and catalogues them as 1748 and 1749.

Additionally, the bright finish type is found as one of two sub-varieties. The more common has the normal reverse, whilst the scarcer type has the smaller reverse design, which can also be distinguished by several key features:

Bright Finish Normal Reverse:

- The rim is slightly thinner than the 'small design' bright finish.
- The two '2's in the date are further apart.
- The second '2' is properly aligned with the other '2'.

Bright Finish Smaller Reverse:

- The rim is thicker than the 'normal' bright finish.
- The two '2's in the date are closer together.
- The second '2' tilts slightly anticlockwise.

Otherwise, this 'small design' has similar features to earlier florin dates, particularly the distance of the left hand sceptre to the 'N' of 'ONE.' The smaller design is catalogued with number 1750 by Davies.

Figure 87 – 1922 Florin Reverses

Bright Finish Normal	**Bright Finish Small**
Thinner rim	Thicker rim
Wider '2's	Closer '2's
'2's aligned	Second '2' turned

1923 Florin:

Major Varieties:

There are two obverses for the 1923 florin (obverse 2 and obverse 3) paired with a single reverse (reverse E) giving the die pairs 2+E and 3+E. The 2+E pairing is considerably rarer than the normal 3+E. Both types have the bright finish and were struck in 50% silver. Davies numbers these 1751 and 1752 respectively.

These two obverses are the same as found on the 1920 florin and details of the differentiators for them can be seen in figures 82-84.

Minor Varieties:

For the rarer 2+E type, which shows the more deeply engraved head, there are specimens which do not have a bright finish, but are in fact dull.

*   *   *   *   *

Denomination: Halfcrown

1911 – 1927

1927 - 1936

Specification: Diameter: 32mm
Weight: 14.1g
Metal: Silver (92.5%) 1911 to 1919
(50%) 1920 to 1936

Obverse Design:

George's bust facing left with abbreviated legend as follows:

1. 'GEORGIVS V DEI GRA: BRITT: OMN: REX' – 1911 to 1926
2. 'GEORGIVS V DEI GRA: BRITT: OMN: REX' – 1926 to 1936
(Modified Effigy)

Reverse Design:

1. For the first reverse, from 1911 to 1927, a crowned shield within a garter. Around the top of the garter, the inscription: 'FID: DEF: IND: IMP:' and around the bottom the word 'HALF CROWN' divided by the date.

The garter itself has the partially obscured inscription 'HONI SOIT QUI' to the left and 'MAL Y PENSE' on the right.

2. For the second reverse, from 1927 (proof only) through to 1936, a shield flanked by interlinked crowned G's. Around the top of the coin, the legend 'FID ♦ DEF IND ♦ IMP' and round the bottom 'HALF ♦ CROWN ♦' followed by the date.

Edge: Milled.

79

Years Produced: 1911 – 1936, for the business strike and proofs from the sets of 1911 and 1927.

Varieties:

Major varieties are known for 1920, 1921, 1922, 1926, 1928 and 1929, whilst minor varieties have been reported for 1911 (proof), 1918, 1919, 1920, 1921, 1925, 1926 and 1933.

For this denomination, there is again no sterling silver issue in 1920 and a 'Modified Effigy' variety occurs for 1926. The 1927 business strike has the earlier reverse whilst the proof has the new design of shield reverse.

1911 Proof Strike Halfcrown:

Major Varieties:

There are no reported major varieties for the 1911 proof strike halfcrown.

Minor Varieties:

The proof strike for 1911 has a single obverse (obverse 1) coupled with a single reverse (reverse A). Davies reports the existence of two minor types of this 1+A die pair, based on the shape of the rim, cataloguing them as 1660 and 1661 respectively. One type has the normal square rim edge and the other has the edge chamfered. Of the two, the chamfered rim is slightly more common.

1918 Halfcrown:

Major Varieties:

There are no major design varieties for the 1918 halfcrown, which has obverse 1 paired with reverse A, and is similar to the halfcrowns from 1911 through to 1920.

Minor Varieties:

The 1918 halfcrown comes as one of two minor varieties. The common type has a normal sized reverse design, whilst the rarer kind has a smaller overall design. Davies catalogues these as numbers 1668 and 1669.

The size of the design is extremely difficult to measure even when specimens of each are available in the hand. The best way to establish the differences by reference to their size is to photograph each, enlarge them so that the coins are equal in size and then measure across the extremities of the legend (not the actual shield part of the design). A good place for measuring is from the bar of the 'F' in 'FID' across to the end of the 'N' in 'CROWN.' Provided that the photographs have been enlarged sufficiently, then the size differences quickly become apparent. Fortunately, there are several more readily available identifiers to distinguish the two types:

Reverse A Type 1 (Normal - larger):

- The second '1' in the date aligns with a border bead. This alignment is of the body of the '1' not the tip which bends slightly.
- The '8' is centred over a space between border beads.
- A thinner rim.

The normal size reverse is also found in one of two sub-types:

1. A normal thinner rim with the lower edge to the crown not struck.
2. A thicker burred edge to the coin and with the lower edge of the crown fully struck.

Reverse A Type 2 (Smaller):

- The second '1' in the date does not align precisely with a border bead, but is nearly centred on a space.
- The '8' is centred over a border bead.
- A thicker 'dimpled' rim.

Figure 88 – 1918 Halfcrown Reverses (1)

Larger Design
'1' to a border bead
'8' centred on a space
Thinner rim

Smaller Design
'1' nearly to a space
'8' centred on a bead
'Thicker rim

The small reverse type occurs as one of three sub-types, differentiated by:

Reverse A Type 2 Small – 1: The second '1' in the date is closer to the buckle and it has a normally spaced '18'.
Reverse A Type 2 Small – 2: The second '1' in the date is closer to the buckle and it has a wider spaced '18'.
Reverse A Type 2 Small – 3: The second '1' and '8' in the date are away from the buckle and it has a normally spaced '18'.

Figure 89 – 1918 Halfcrown Reverses (2)

Small Type 1	**Small Type 2**	**Small Type 3**
'1' close to buckle	'1' close to buckle	'1' away from buckle
'8' close to buckle	'8' close to buckle	'8' away from buckle
Normal spaced '18'	Wider spaced '18'	Normal spaced '18'

The 'dimpled' rim which is characteristic of the small reverse is quite clearly visible in the photographs of the type 2 and type 3 reverses.

1919 Halfcrown:

Major Varieties:

There are no major design varieties for the 1919 halfcrown, which has obverse 1 paired with reverse A, and is similar to the halfcrowns from 1911 through to 1920.

Minor Varieties:

As for 1918, the 1919 halfcrown comes as one of two minor varieties. The common type has a normal sized reverse design, whilst the rarer kind has a smaller overall design. The best way to measure the sizes of the reverse is to use photography, as described for the 1918 halfcrown. These two types are numbered 1670 and 1671 respectively by Davies.

Fortunately, there are several more readily available identifiers to distinguish the two types:

Reverse A Type 1 (Normal - Larger):

- The first '1' in the date is of normal length.
- The '9's are normal as measured by the gap between the tail of the '9' and the base of the '1'.
- The gap between the first '19' and the buckle is narrow.

Reverse A Type 2 (Smaller):

- The first '1' in the date is slightly shorter.
- The '9's are more upright as measured by the gap between the tail of the '9' and the base of the '1'.
- The gap between the first '19' and the buckle is wider.

Figure 90 – 1919 Halfcrown Reverses

Larger Reverse	**Small Reverse**
The '1' is normal	The '1' is smaller
The '9's are normal	The '9's are more upright
Large gap tail of '9' to '1'	Small gap tail of '9' to '1'
Small gap '19's to buckle	Larger gap '19's to buckle

1920 Halfcrown:

Major Varieties:

There are five major varieties for the 1920 halfcrown. This date has three obverses (obverses 1, 2 and 3) and two reverses (reverses A and B) but these are not fully paired, since there is no 2+B type, leaving 1+A, 1+B, 2+A, 3+A and 3+B types. Davies catalogues these five types with numbers 1672 – 1676 respectively.

Obverses:

Obverse 1: This obverse is the one found on all the earlier halfcrowns in the George V series, from 1911 to 1919 and can be identified by:

- A small head, measuring 24mm.
- The effigy is in high relief.
- The letters in 'REX' are close spaced.
- The 'I' of 'DEI' points to a space.
- The 'A' of 'GRA' points to a bead.
- The 'I' of 'BRITT' points to the right of a bead.
- The gap between the bases of the 'A' and the 'B' above the head is wide.
- There is normal hair to the back of the head.
- There are 185 rim beads.

Obverse 2:

- A medium head, measuring 24½mm.
- The effigy is in high relief.
- The letters in 'REX' are wide spaced.
- The 'I' of 'DEI' points to a border bead (more correctly to the right of a bead).
- The 'A' of 'GRA' points to a space between beads.
- The 'I' of 'BRITT' points to a bead.
- The gap between the bases of the 'A' and the 'B' above the head is narrower.
- There is better defined hair to the back of the head.

83

- There are 188 rim beads.

Obverse 2 is also described as having a thinner obverse legend than obverse 1. This is most noticeable in the thickness of the 'I' in 'BRITT'. Also, obverse 2 is struck slightly off-centre, which shows as a thicker rim around 'REX' in the legend and a thinner one around 'DEI'. These features can be seen in figures 94, 91 and 92 respectively.

Obverse 3:

- A larger head, measuring 25mm.
- The effigy is in low relief.
- The letters in 'REX' are wide spaced.
- The 'I' of 'DEI' points to a border bead (more correctly to the right of a bead).
- The 'A' of 'GRA' points to right of a bead.
- The 'I' of 'BRITT' points to a bead.
- The gap between the bases of the 'A' and the 'B' above the head is narrower.
- There is normal hair to the back of the neck.
- There are 188 rim beads.

The size of the head is extremely difficult to measure and the depth of the strike is only really useful for differentiating high grade examples. Equally, the quality of the hair to the back of the neck is only visible on high grade examples. Fortunately, these three features are not the only differences between obverse 2 and obverse 3, as the pointing of the 'A' in 'GRA' can be used definitively.

Figure 91 – 1920 Halfcrown Obverses (1)

Obverse 1	Obverses 2&3
Narrow Rex	Wider Rex

Figure 92 – 1920 Halfcrown Obverses (2)

Obverse 1	Obverses 2&3
'I' of 'DEI' to a space	'I' of 'DEI' to a bead

Figure 93 – 1920 Halfcrown Obverses (3)

Obverse 1	**Obverse 2**	**Obverse 3**
'A' of 'GRA'	'A' of 'GRA'	'A' of 'GRA'
to a bead	to a space	to right of bead

Figure 94 – 1920 Halfcrown Obverses (4)

Obverse 1	**Obverse 2 &3**
'I' of 'BRITT'	'I' of 'BRITT'
to right of bead	to a bead

Figure 95 – 1920 Halfcrown Obverses (5)

Obverse 1	**Obverses 2&3**
Wide gap 'A: B' to head	Narrow gap 'A: B' to head

Figure 96 – 1920 Halfcrown Obverses (6)

Obverses 1& 3	**Obverses 2**
Normal hair	Well-defined hair

85

Reverses:

The differences in the reverses A and B are very slight and scarcely justify them being regarded as major varieties. However, Davies catalogues them as A and B, and they are regarded in the same way here for the sake of consistency.

Reverse A: Reverse A can be identified by:

- The design is normal sized.
- There is a raised edge on the garter above the 'F' of 'HALF' and the '19'.
- There is no pocket above the 'C' of 'CROWN'.
- A thinner edge.

Reverse B: Reverse B is characterised by:

- The design is slightly smaller.
- There is a plain edge on the garter above the 'F' of 'HALF and the '19'.
- There is a small pocket above the 'C' of 'CROWN'.
- A thicker edge.

According to Davies this reverse has a die crack at 3 o'clock. However, there are specimens known without the crack.

As for the 1918 and 1919 halfcrowns, the best way to measure the size of the reverses is to use photography, as described for the 1918 halfcrown.

Figure 96 – 1920 Halfcrown Reverses (1)

Reverse A	**Reverse B**
Raised edge to garter above 'F'	Plain edge to garter above 'F'
Thinner edge	Thicker edge

Figure 97 – 1920 Halfcrown Reverses (2)

Reverse A	**Reverse B**
No pocket above 'C'	Pocket above 'C'

Minor Varieties:

Obverses:

Coins with obverse 1 when paired with reverse A are found in one of a number of minor varieties:

Obverse 1+A – 1: Early strikes which are often found with a concave edge, which leaves the border beads indistinct. This type also has a normal dull finish.
Obverse 1+A – 2: Later strikes which are flatter with distinct border beads and also have a dull finish.
Obverse 1+A – 3: Some later strikes are found with a bright finish.

Obverse 2 paired with reverse A does not appear to have any minor types.

As for obverse 1, there are a number of varieties for obverse 3 coins, based on the die pairing 3+A.

Obverse 3+A – 1: 'Normal' coins which have a dull finish.
Obverse 3+A – 2: Some specimens are known with a bright finish.
Obverse 3+A – 3: Some examples of the dull finish type have a thicker obverse rim and tiny border beads.

Reverses:

When paired with obverse 1, there are two types of reverse B, giving minor varieties of the 1+B major variety.

Reverse 1+B Type 1: The 'normal' reverse B has standard sized beads, the standard wide rim and a wide gap between the legend and the edge.
Reverse 1+B Type 2: These coins show rather smaller beads, a thinner rim and a narrower gap between the edge and legend.

Figure 99 – 1920 Halfcrown Reverses (3)

Reverse B1	Reverse B2
Normal size beads	Smaller beads
Normal thicker edge	Thinner edge
Normal gap to legend	Narrower gap to legend

1921 Halfcrown:

Major Varieties:

There are two reported major varieties for the 1921 halfcrown. This date has a single obverse (obverse 3) and two reverses (reverses B and C), giving the die pairs 3+B and 3+C and catalogued by Davies as 1677 and 1678. However, the identifiers for distinguishing these two types are mostly few and difficult to see with the naked eye.

Reverse B: This is the rarer reverse and is identified as having:

- The second '1' in '1921' pointing to a space between border beads. This refers to the body of the '1' not the tip which curves away to the left.
- The reverse design is smaller than reverse C.

Reverse C:

- The second '1' in '1921' points to a border bead.
- The reverse design is slightly larger than reverse B.

As for earlier halfcrowns, the only certain way to establish the size of the reverses is through photography, careful sizing of the images and measuring of the width of the design.

Figure 100 – 1921 Halfcrown Reverses (1)

Reverse B	**Reverse C**
Second '1' to a space	Second '1' to a bead

Minor varieties:

The 3+C major variety is found as one of two minor varieties. The differences which relate to the reverse are defined as:

Reverse C Type 1: Normal reverse C (Davies 1678), has a larger design than reverse B and also has the 'O' in 'HONI' with a narrow lower loop.

Reverse C Type 2: The larger design reverse C, has the whole design a fraction of a millimetre larger than both reverse B and the more common reverse C1. This type is catalogued by Davies with number 1679.

The differences between C1 and C2 are difficult to decide for a specific coin without using photography. However, the 'O' in 'HONI' has an even loop all round and is a clear differentiator.

Figure 101 – 1921 Halfcrown Reverses (2)

Reverse C1
Thin lower loop

Reverse C2
Even loop all round

1922 Halfcrown:

Major Varieties:

There are two reported major varieties for the 1922 halfcrown. This date has a single obverse (obverse 3) and two reverses (reverses C and D), giving the die pairs 3+C and 3+D.

Reverse C: This is described as having the reverse of 1921.

- The colon after 'DEF' points to a border bead.
- The bottom dot of the colon after 'DEF', when viewed perpendicular to the curve of the crown, is above the space between two crown pearls.
- The 'F' of 'FID' points to a border bead.
- The crown touches the top of the shield.
- The 'H' in 'HALF' is smaller.
- The cross on the top of the crown points to a bead.
- There are 189 border beads.
- The left leg of the 'N' in 'CROWN' points to a border bead.
- The 'D' of 'DEF' points to a border bead.

Reverse D: This is described as having the reverse of 1923.

- The colon after 'DEF' points to a space between border beads.
- The bottom dot of the colon after 'DEF' is above a crown pearl.
- The 'F' of 'FID' points to a space between border beads, although more properly to the left of a bead.
- There is a groove or gap between the crown and the top of the shield.
- The 'H' in 'HALF' is taller.
- The cross on the top of the crown points to the right of a bead.
- There are 190 border beads.
- The left leg of the 'N' in 'CROWN' points to a space between beads.
- The 'D' of 'DEF' points to the left of a bead.

Figure 102 – 1922 Halfcrown Reverses (1)

Reverse C
Colon to bead
Lower dot over a space

Reverse D
Colon to space
Lower dot over a pearl

Figure 103 – 1922 Halfcrown Reverses (2)

Reverse C
'F' to a bead

Reverse D
'F' to space

Figure 104 – 1922 Halfcrown Reverses (3)

Reverse C
No groove
crown to shield

Reverse D
Groove
crown to shield

Figure 105 – 1922 Halfcrown Reverses (4)

Reverse C
Smaller 'H'

Reverse D
Taller 'H'

Figure 106 – 1922 Halfcrown Reverses (5)

Reverse C
Cross to a bead

Reverse D
Cross to right of a bead

Figure 107 – 1922 Halfcrown Reverses (6)

Reverse C
Left leg of 'N' to a bead

Reverse D
Left leg of 'N' to a space

Figure 108 – 1922 Halfcrown Reverses (7)

Reverse C
'D' to a bead

Reverse D
'D' to left of bead

Both the 3+C and 3+D types are found with a matt finish or a bright finish. The 3+D in matt finish is the rarest of the varieties with the bright finish 3+C next. The 3+C matt and 3+D bright are about equally common.

Overall, therefore, there are 4 different major types of 1922 halfcrown. These are catalogued by Davies with numbers 1680, 1681, 1682 and 1683.

Minor Varieties:

There are no reported minor varieties for this date.

1925 Halfcrown:

Major Varieties:

There are no reported major varieties for the 1925 halfcrown.

Minor Varieties:

The 1925 halfcrown has a single obverse (obverse 3) coupled with a single reverse (reverse D). Davies reports the existence of two minor types of this 3+D die pair, based on the shape of the rim. One type has the normal square rim edge and the other has the edge chamfered. Of the two, the chamfered rim is slightly less common, although overall any 1925 halfcrown, especially in high grade, is scarce. Davies catalogues the normal edge as number 1686 and the chamfered rim as 1687.

1926 Halfcrown:

Major Varieties:

Like several other silver denominations, the 1926 halfcrown has two obverse types (obverses 3 and 4), which are paired with a single reverse (reverse D) giving the die pairs 3+D and 4+D. Obverse 3 is the obverse found on halfcrowns between 1920 and 1925, whilst obverse 4 is the well known 'Modified Effigy' type.

Obverses:

Obverse 3: This obverse can be identified by:

- Narrower rim than the ME obverse.
- The 'I' of 'DEI' points to the right of a border bead.
- The border beads are small and rounded.
- The initials 'BM' on the truncation are towards the centre of the neck, and have two dots after them.
- The king has straight eyelids.
- The eye has no pupil.
- Horizontal under side to the nose.
- More border beads than obverse 4.

Obverse 4: This is the well-known 'Modified Effigy' or 'ME' type, distinguished by:

- Slightly wider rim.
- The 'I' of 'DEI' points to a space between border beads.
- The border beads are larger and elongated.
- The most famous identifier: the position of the initials of Sir Bertram Mackennal (BM) on the neck truncation. These are found much further back on the neck and are without dots.

- The king's eyelids curve down.
- The eye has a distinct pupil.
- The underside of the nose curves slightly.
- Less border beads than obverse 3.

Although the identifiers are broadly the same as for the other denominations, there are several which are different and do not translate from one denomination to another.

Figure 109 – 1926 Halfcrown Obverses (1)

Obverse 3	**Obverse 4**
Thin rim	Wider rim
'I' of 'DEI' to right of bead	'I' of 'DEI' points to a space
Small round border beads	Large elongated border beads

Figure 110 – 1926 Halfcrown Obverses (2)

Obverse 3	**Obverse 4**
Ordinary Effigy	Modified Effigy
'BM' near centre	'BM' to the rear
'BM' has dots	'BM' has no dots

Figure 111 – 1926 Halfcrown Obverses (3)

Obverse 5	**Obverse 6**
Ordinary Effigy	Modified Effigy
Straight Eyelid	Curved Eyelid
No Eyeball	Eyeball
Straight Underside to Nose	Curved Underside to Nose

Minor Varieties:

There are no minor design varieties for the 1926 halfcrown. However, there is an error type of the obverse 3 coin which has achieved the status of a variety. This was caused by a blocked die and resulted in some specimens being struck with an incomplete colon after 'OMN.' In some cases, either the upper or lower colon dot is missing, whilst in others the entire colon is absent. The type missing the entire colon is catalogued by Davies with number 1689.

Figure 112 – 1926 Halfcrown Obverse (4)

Obverse 3
Missing colon dot

1928 Halfcrown:

Major Varieties:

The 1928 halfcrown has the new reverse design, first introduced in the proof set of 1927. This year sees three major varieties. There are two obverses found (obverse 1 and obverse 2) and two reverses (reverse B and reverse C). However, the die pairs are not fully meshed, with pairings 1+B, 2+B and 1+C found. Davies catalogues these three types with numbers 1701, 1702 and 1703 respectively.

Obverses:

Obverse 1:

- The king has an indented shallow forehead.
- The effigy has a prominent eyebrow.
- The coin has a thinner rim.
- The effigy is shallow.

Obverse 2: This is described as being struck from the modified effigy puncheon.

- The king has a flat full forehead.
- The effigy has a shallow eyebrow.
- The coin has a thicker rim.
- The effigy is in higher relief.

High grade specimens of the higher effigy type can be more readily distinguished from obverse 1 by placing the coin obverse down on a perfectly flat surface, where it will be found to 'rock' slightly.

94

Figure 113 – 1928 Halfcrown Obverses

Obverse 1
Indented forehead
Prominent eyebrow

Obverse 2
Full forehead
Smaller eyebrow

Reverses:

Reverse B:

- The 'D' of 'FID' points to a space.
- The 'D' of 'DEF' points to a border bead.
- The gap between the petals of the rose at the top of the obverse points to the left of a border bead.
- The 'I' of 'IMP' points to a border bead.
- The 'I' of 'IND' points to a border bead.
- The 'D' of 'IND' points to a border bead.
- The tip of the '9' in the date ends over a bead.
- There are 157 border beads.

Reverse C:

- The 'D' of 'FID' points to the right of a border bead.
- The 'D' of 'DEF' points to the right of a bead.
- The gap between the petals of the rose at the top of the obverse points to a border bead.
- The 'I' of 'IMP' points to the right of a border bead.
- The 'I' of 'IND' points to the left of a border tooth.
- The 'D' of 'IND' points to a space between border beads.
- The tip of the '9' ends over a space between beads.
- There are 158 border beads.

Figure 114 – 1928 Halfcrown Reverses (1)

Reverse B
'D' points to a space

Reverse C
'D' points to right of bead

95

Figure 115 – 1928 Halfcrown Reverses (2)

Reverse B
'D' of 'DEF' to bead

Reverse C
'D' of 'DEF' to right of bead

Figure 116 – 1928 Halfcrown Reverses (3)

Reverse B
Petal gap to left of bead

Reverse C
Petal gap to bead

Figure 117 – 1928 Halfcrown Reverses (4)

Reverse B
'I' points to a border bead

Reverse C
'I' points to right of bead

Figure 118 – 1928 Halfcrown Reverses (5)

Reverse B
'I' points to a bead
'D' points to a bead

Reverse C
'I' points to right of bead
'D' points to a space

Figure 119 – 1928 Halfcrown Reverses (6)

Reverse B	**Reverse C**
Tip of '9' over a bead	Tip of '9' over a space

Minor Varieties:

There are no reported minor varieties for this date.

1929 Halfcrown:

Major Varieties:

The 1929 halfcrown has a single obverse (obverse 1) and two reverses (reverse D and reverse E), giving the die pairings 1+D and 1+E, catalogued by Davies as numbers 1704 and 1705.

Reverses:

Reverse D:

- The 'D' of 'DEF' points to a space.
- The 'E' of 'DEF' points to the left of a border bead.
- The 'I' of 'IND' points to the right of a border tooth.
- The 'D' of 'IND' points to a space between border beads.
- The 'D' of 'FID' points to a space.
- The 'I' of 'IMP' points to the right of a border bead.
- The gap between the petals of the rose at the top of the obverse points to a border bead.
- There are 157 border beads.

Reverse E:

- The 'D' of 'DEF' points to the left of a border bead.
- The 'E' of 'DEF' points to the right of a border bead.
- The 'I' of 'IND' points to the left of a border bead.
- The 'D' of 'IND' points to a border bead.
- The 'D' of 'FID' points to a border bead.
- The 'I' of 'IMP' points to the left of a border bead.
- The gap between the petals of the rose at the top of the obverse points to a space between border beads.
- There are 158 border beads.

97

Figure 120 – 1929 Halfcrown Reverses (1)

Reverse D	**Reverse E**
'D' of 'DEF' to a space	'D' of 'DEF' to left of a bead
'E' of 'DEF' to left of a bead	'E' of 'DEF' to right of a bead

Figure 121 – 1929 Halfcrown Reverses (2)

Reverse D	**Reverse E**
'I' of 'IND' to right of a bead	'I' of 'IND' to left of a bead
'D' of 'IND' to a space	'D' of 'IND' to a bead

Figure 122 – 1929 Halfcrown Reverses (3)

Reverse D	**Reverse E**
'D' of 'FID' to a space	'D' of 'FID' to a bead

Figure 123 – 1929 Halfcrown Reverses (4)

Reverse D	**Reverse E**
'I' of 'IMP' to right of a bead	'I' of 'IMP' to left of a bead

Figure 124 – 1929 Halfcrown Reverses (5)

Reverse D
Petal gap to a bead

Reverse E
Petal gap to space

Minor Varieties:

There are no reported minor varieties for the 1929 halfcrown.

1933 Halfcrown:

Major Varieties:

There are no reported major varieties for the 1933 halfcrown.

Minor Varieties:

The 1933 halfcrown has a single obverse (obverse 1) coupled with the single reverse (reverse E). However, the major type is found as one of two minor varieties for this year, differentiated by the overall size of the design. Davies distinguishes these two types, cataloguing them with numbers 1709 and 1710.

Reverse E Type 1 (Normal):

- The reverse design as measured across the coin from the outer edge of the legend to outer edge of the legend is 28mm.
- The edge is thicker.

Reverse E Type 2 (Larger):

- The reverse design as measured across the coin from the outer edge of the legend to outer edge of the legend is 28.5mm.
- The edge is thinner.

The width of the edge is the clearest means of identifying the two types whilst photography is the only practical means of telling two specimens apart based on the size of the design.

Figure 125 – 1933 Halfcrown Reverses

Normal Reverse E1
Thicker rim

Larger Reverse E2
Thin rim

*   *   *   *   *

Denomination: Crown

1927(Proof) – 1936

1935

Specification: Diameter: 39mm
Weight: 28.3g
Metal: Silver (50%)

Obverse Design:

George's bust facing left with abbreviated legend as follows:

1. 'GEORGIVS V DEI GRA: BRITT: OMN: REX' – 1927 to 1936 (except 1935)
2. 'GEORGIVS V. DG. BRITT: OMN: REX. FD. IND: IMP:' – 1935

Reverse Design:

1. For the first reverse, a large crown with the date above, within a wreath and known as the wreath crown. Around the top of the wreath, the inscription: '♦FID ♦ ♦ DEF ♦ ♦ IND ♦ ♦ IMP♦' and around the bottom the word '♦ CROWN ♦'.

2. For the second reverse, the 'art deco' style St George and the dragon, with the word 'CROWN 1935' around the top.

Edge: 1927 – 1936 - Milled.
1935 – incuse inscription 'DECUS ET TUTAMEN ANNO REGNI XXV'

Years Produced: 1928 – 1936, except 1935, for the wreath crown ordinary strike and a proof in 1927 from the set. For the art deco style crown, these are a one-year type, struck in 1935 only.

Varieties:

There are no reported varieties for the wreath crown series, whilst the 1935 type, both business and proof strikes, has a number of minor types, including edge errors.

1935 Business Strike Crown:

Major Varieties:

The vast majority of 1935 crowns have obverse 1, paired with reverse A, but rarely specimens are found with a different reverse, designated reverse B.

Reverses:

Reverse A:

This is the very common reverse and is characterised by the pointing of the sword point, which is to a border bead. Reverse A is numbered 1650 by Davies.

Reverse B:

This is the very much rarer reverse and is identified by the pointing of the sword point, which is to a space between border beads. Reverse B is numbered 1654 by Davies, but is designated as unconfirmed.

Figure 126 – 1935 Crown Reverses

<table>
<tr><td align="center">Reverse A
Sword point to a bead</td><td align="center">Reverse B
Sword points to a space between beads</td></tr>
</table>

There are also two different strike qualities. Many of the business strike coins were struck from standard dies, but a smaller number were produced in what is described as a 'specimen' finish. These were struck because the demand for the raised edge proof coins was not satisfied by the Mint and a better quality normal strike in a red presentation box was produced. The differences between the normal currency issue and the specimen type are difficult to describe as they simply relate to the sharpness of the finish and the appearance of the flan of the final coin. However, the specimen coin has a prooflike field and when set by a normal strike is immediately obvious.

Minor Varieties:

The common 1935 crown with die pairing 1+A has no design varieties identified. However, there is an error to the edge inscription that occurred and which is now regarded as a variety in its own right. Thus the edge can read:

Edge Variety 1: DECUS ET TUTAMEN ANNO REGNI XXV – The standard coin.
Edge Variety 2:   MEN ANNO REGNI XXV
                                – Missing 'DECUS ET TUTA'

The latter type is numbered 1652 by Davies. The coins are also struck with the incuse edge inscription the correct way up or upside down in respect of the obverse.

1935 Proof Strike Crown:

Major Varieties:

There are two kinds of proof strike crown, the more common having a raised edge inscription and struck in sterling (92.5%) silver and the other much rarer being a proof version of the common business strike i.e. with an incuse edge inscription. Like the business strike, the incuse edge proof is described with the die pairings 1+A and 1+B and can be identified from the pointing of St George's sword, as in figure 126. However, in this case, unlike for the business strike, it is the 1+A version which is shown as unconfirmed by Davies.

The incuse edge proof crown is also found in both 50% and 92.5% sterling silver. These can be distinguished from each other by the 'ring' when struck, although this is an action to be undertaken with care given the value and quality of strike for this coin. Debased silver gives a higher note than sterling silver.

There are no identified major varieties of the raised edge proof coin.

Minor Varieties:

There are no known minor design varieties of the raised edge proof crown. However, like the business strike there is a rare edge error type where the lettering reads:

'DECUS ANNO REGNI ET TUTAMEN VVX'

For the rare incuse edge proof, these can be found with consistently sized edge lettering or with thinner letters in places. It is not clear whether the thin lettering is found on either the debased silver strike, the sterling silver strike, or both.

*   *   *   *   *

George VI

Period: 1936 - 1952

Denomination: Threepence

1937 – 1945

Specification: Diameter: 16mm
Weight: 1.4g
Metal: Silver (50%) 1937 to 1945 (last year of issue)

Obverse Design:

George's bust facing left with abbreviated legend as follows:

'GEORGIVS VI D : G : BR : OMN : REX' – 1937 to 1945

Reverse Design:

The shield of St George lying on a Tudor rose, which divides the date. The inscription 'FID : DEF : IND : IMP' around the top of the coin and the words 'THREE · PENCE' around the bottom.

Edge: Plain

Years Produced: 1937 to 1945, plus a proof in the set of 1937. Most of the 1945 issue were melted down by the Mint, making this an extremely rare date.

Varieties:

The only year where there is a major variety is in 1937 for the business strike, and even this is noted as unconfirmed by Davies.

1937 Business Strike Threepence:

Major Varieties:

The common 1937 threepence has obverse 1 paired with reverse A. The unconfirmed major variety also has obverse 1, but is paired with reverse B, which is found on all the other dates in this series up to and including 1945.

104

Reverses:

Reverse A:

- The 'I' of 'IMP' points to a border bead.
- The 'P' of 'IMP' points to a space between beads.

Reverse B:

- The 'I' of 'IMP' points to a space between border beads.
- The 'P' of 'IMP' points to a bead.

Figure 127 – 1937 Threepence Reverses

Reverse A	**Reverse B**
'I' of 'IMP' points to a bead	'I' of 'IMP' points to a space
'P' of 'IMP' points to a space	'P' of 'IMP' points to a bead

Minor Varieties:

There are no reported minor varieties for the 1937 threepence.

*   *   *   *   *

Denomination: Sixpence

1937 – 1952

1937 – 1948   1949 - 1952

Specification: Diameter: 19mm
Weight: 3.0g
Metal: Silver (50%) 1937 to 1946
Cupronickel 1947 to 1952

Obverse Design:

George's bust facing left with abbreviated legend as follows:

'GEORGIVS VI D : G : BR : OMN : REX' – 1937 to 1952

Reverse Design:

1. For reverse A, struck between 1937 and 1948, the letters 'GRI' (Georgius Rex Imperator) crowned and dividing the date, with the inscription 'FID·DEF· ·IND·IMP' around the top and 'SIXPENCE' around the bottom. Also, the small letters 'KG' underneath 'GRI' and above 'SIXPENCE.'

2. For the second reverse, from 1949 onwards, the letters 'GVIR' dividing the date, topped by a crown and with the legend '·FID DEF·' around the top and '·SIXPENCE·' around the bottom.

Edge: Milled.

Years Produced: 1937 to 1952, plus proofs in the sets of 1937, 1950 and 1951.

Varieties:

For this date run there are no reported design varieties, but there are unconfirmed reports of specimens for 1946 being struck in cupronickel as well as in debased silver.

*   *   *   *   *

106

Denomination: Shilling

1937 – 1951

English Reverse

1937 – 1948   1949 – 1951

Scottish Reverse

1937 – 1948   1949 – 1951

Specification: Diameter: 24mm
Weight: 5.7g
Metal: Silver (50%) 1937 to 1946
Cupronickel 1947 to 1951

Obverse Design:

George's bust facing left with abbreviated legend as follows:

'GEORGIVS VI D : G : BR : OMN : REX' – 1937 to 1951

Reverse Design:

There are two types of reverse for this series: The English reverse and Scottish type. Both types were altered in 1949 to remove the inscription 'IND IMP' following Indian independence.

1. For the English reverse A, struck between 1937 and 1948, the design includes a lion on a crown dividing the date, with the words 'FID DEF IND IMP' around the top of the coin and the words 'ONE SHILLING' around the bottom.

2. Reverse B of the English shilling, struck from 1949 to 1951 is similar in design to reverse A, but omits 'IND IMP' and has 'FID' to the left and 'DEF' to the right.

3. For the Scottish reverse A, struck between 1937 and 1948, the design includes a facing lion on a crown dividing the date, and with the St Andrew's cross on the left and a thistle on the right. The legend is as for the English type above.

4. Reverse B of the Scottish shilling, struck between 1949 and 1951 is similar in design to the Scottish reverse A, but, as for the English shilling, omits 'IND IMP' and has 'FID' to the left and 'DEF' to the right.

Edge: Milled.

Years Produced: 1937 to 1951, plus proofs in the sets of 1937, 1950 and 1951, for both the English and Scottish shillings.

Varieties:

Major varieties exist for just the 1946 English type. Additionally, there is an error coin variety for the 1943 English shilling and a possible major variety of the 1946 Scottish type based on the alloy used.

1943 English Shilling:

Major Varieties:

There are no known design varieties of the 1943 English shilling. However, the normal alignment of the obverse/reverse on this series of coins is en medaille i.e. the obverse and reverse are both the same way up. Some coins of the English 1943 shilling were struck in error with the die axis inverted. These are described by Davies and are catalogued as numbers 2116 and 2117.

Minor Varieties:

There are no minor varieties for this denomination and date.

1946 English Shilling:

Major Varieties:

The English shillings from 1937 up to 1946 all have a single obverse (obverse 1) paired with a single reverse (reverse A). During 1946 a small change was made to the reverse, designated reverse B, but still paired to obverse 1, giving die pairs for 1946 of 1+A and 1+B. These two types are catalogued by Davies as numbers 2120 and 2121. Reverse B is then found on the remaining shillings in this series up to 1951.

Reverses:

Reverse A:

- The rim is narrow.
- The 'I' of 'IND' points to a space between beads.
- The first 'I' of 'SHILLING' points to a space between beads and the second to a bead.
- The overall design of the crown, lion and legend is large.

Reverse B:

- The rim is wider.
- The 'I' of 'IND' points to a bead.
- The first 'I' of 'SHILLING' points to a bead and the second to a space.
- The overall design of the crown, lion and legend is slightly smaller.

Figure 128 – 1946 English Shilling Reverses (1)

Reverse A	**Reverse B**
Narrow rim	Wider rim
'I' of 'IND' points to a space	'I' of 'IND' points to a bead

Figure 129 – 1946 English Shilling Reverses (2)

Reverse A	**Reverse B**
1st 'I' to a space	1st 'I' to a bead
2nd 'I' to a bead	2nd 'I' to a space

Checking the design size is difficult, enlarging photographs being the best option in the absence of precise measuring equipment. However, the other identifiers are much simpler to use definitively. It is also noticeable that there are differences in the size and shape of the border beads on the two types.

There are also unconfirmed reports of some 1946 English shillings struck in cupronickel, presumably as a trial in readiness for the changeover from debased silver to cupronickel from 1947.

The two kinds are readily distinguishable, as the cupronickel type has a darker steely grey finish.

Minor Varieties:

There are no reported minor varieties for this year and type.

1946 Scottish Shilling:

Major Varieties:

As for the sixpence and the English shilling, there are unconfirmed reports of a 1946 Scottish shilling struck in cupronickel, instead of the usual 50% silver.

Minor Varieties:

There are no reported minor varieties for this year and type.

*　　*　　*　　*　　*

Denomination: Florin

1937 – 1951

1937 – 1948   1949 – 1951

Specification: Diameter: 28.5mm
Weight: 11.3g
Metal: Silver (50%) 1937 to 1946
Cupronickel 1947 to 1951

Obverse Design:

George's bust facing left with abbreviated legend as follows:

'GEORGIVS VI D : G : BR : OMN : REX' – 1937 to 1951

Reverse Design:

1. For reverse A, struck between 1937 and 1948, a crowned rose, flanked on either side by a thistle and a shamrock and with the letter G below the thistle and R below the shamrock. Around the top of the coin is the inscription ':FID:DEF: :IND:IMP:' and around the bottom the words ':TWO SHILLINGS:' followed by the date.

2. For the second reverse, from 1949 onwards, the overall design is similar but the words 'IND IMP' are omitted and the lower inscription and date are more widely spread out.

Edge: Milled.

Years Produced: 1937 to 1951, plus proofs in the sets of 1937, 1950 and 1951.

Varieties:

For this date run there is a major variety for 1937, based on a small design change and another unconfirmed in 1946, where there is an alloy change. There are no

111

reported minor varieties for any dates in this series.

1937 Business Strike Florin:

The business strike florin has a single obverse (obverse 1) paired with one of two reverses (reverse A and reverse B) giving the varieties 1+A and 1+B.

Reverse A:

- The second 'I' in 'SHILLINGS' points to border bead. Some sources describe this as being nearly to a bead.
- The 'D' of 'IND' points to a bead.
- There are 146 border beads.
- The left leg of the 'N' in 'IND' points to a border bead.

Reverse B:

- The second 'I' in 'SHILLINGS' points to a space between border beads.
- The 'D' of 'IND' points to a space between beads.
- There are 144 border beads.
- The left leg of the 'N' in 'IND' points to a space between border beads.

Figure 130 – 1937 Florin Reverses (1)

| **Reverse A** | **Reverse B** |
| 'I' of 'SHILLINGS' to a bead | 'I' of 'SHILLINGS' to a space |

Figure 131 – 1937 Florin Reverses (2)

Reverse A
'D' of 'IND' to a bead
Left leg of 'N' to bead

Reverse B
'D' of 'IND' to a space
Left leg of 'N' to a space

1946 Florin:

Major Varieties:

As for the lower denominations, there are unconfirmed reports of a 1946 florin struck in cupronickel, instead of the normal 50% silver.

Minor Varieties:

There are no reported minor varieties for this year and type.

*   *   *   *   *

Denomination: Halfcrown

1937 – 1952

1937 – 1948

1949 – 1952

Specification: Diameter: 32mm
Weight: 14.1g
Metal: Silver (50%) 1937 to 1946
Cupronickel 1947 to 1952

Obverse Design:

George's bust facing left with abbreviated legend as follows:

'GEORGIVS VI D : G : BR : OMN : REX' – 1937 to 1952

Reverse Design:

1. A large shield with interlinked G's topped by crowns on either side, and the inscription 'FID:DEF IND:IMP' around the top and around the bottom the words 'HALF CROWN' followed by the date.

2. For the second reverse, from 1949 onwards, the overall design is similar but the words 'IND IMP' are omitted and the lower inscription and date are more widely spread out.

Edge: Milled.

Years Produced: 1937 to 1952, plus proofs in the sets of 1937, 1950 and 1951.

114

Varieties:

For this date run there are no reported design varieties, but there is an unconfirmed type for 1946 based on the alloy used.

1946 Half Crown:

Major Varieties:

For this date there are no reported design varieties, but as for other denominations, there are unconfirmed reports of specimens for 1946 being struck in cupronickel as well as in debased silver.

Minor Varieties:

There are no reported minor varieties for this year and type.

*   *   *   *   *

Denomination: Crown

1937

1951

Specification: Diameter: 39mm
Weight: 28.3g
Metal: Silver (50%) 1937
Cupronickel 1951

Obverse Designs:

George's bust facing left with abbreviated legend as follows:

1. 'GEORGIVS VI D : G : BR : OMN : REX' – 1937
2. 'GEORGIVS VI D:G:BR:OMN:REX F:D: FIVE SHILLINGS' – 1951 Proof

Reverse Designs:

1. The royal arms, crowned and supported by a lion and a unicorn with the inscription 'FID:DEF: :IND:IMP' around the top and around the bottom the words 'CROWN : 1937'.

2. For the 'Festival of Britain' crown of 1951, the 'St George and the Dragon' design of Benedetto Pistrucci with the date underneath in the exergue.

Edges:

1. The edge of the 1937 crown is milled.
2. The edge of the 1951 crown is plain with the incuse legend 'MDCCCLI CIVIUM INDUSTRIA FLORET CIVITAS MCMLI'.

The incuse legend may be either way up in relation to the obverse of the coin.

Years Produced: 1937 for both a business and proof strike and 1951 for the proof, either as a single coin or from the sets.

Varieties:

There are no design varieties for either date. However, there is a packaging variety for the 1951 proof and an edge error type for the same year. Both years also have varieties based on the type of proof finish.

1937 Proof Strike Crown:

Major Varieties:

There are three variants of the 1937 proof crown:

1. The 'standard' proof from the set.
2. A heavily frosted proof, possibly in sterling, rather than debased silver.
3. A superior proof from sandblasted dies.

The latter are particularly rare.

Minor Varieties:

For this date there are no reported minor varieties.

1951 Proof Strike Crown:

Major Varieties:

As for 1937, there are three varieties of the 1951 proof crown:

1. The 'standard' proof either boxed or from the set.
2. A heavily frosted proof, with finer edge lettering than the standard coin.
3. A superior proof from sandblasted dies.

Again, the latter are particularly rare.

Minor Varieties:

The single crown was issued by the mint in its own presentation box, which may be either green or red in colour and have a pull off or sliding lid. The latter type is the scarcer of the two.

Also, a very few coins were struck in error, without the incuse edge inscription, giving them a plain edge. A second error coin with a blundered Latin date and a larger space before 'FLORET' has also been reported.

*   *   *   *   *

Elizabeth II

Period: 1953 - 1970

Denomination: Sixpence

1953   1954 -1970

1953 – 1970

Specification: Diameter: 19mm
Weight: 3.0g
Metal: Cupronickel: Copper 75%
Nickel 25%

Obverse Design:

Elizabeth's bust facing right with abbreviated legend as follows:

1. 'ELIZABETH II DEI GRATIA BRITT:OMN:REGINA + ' – 1953 only
2. 'ELIZABETH · II · DEI · GRATIA · REGINA + ' – 1954 to 1970

Reverse Design:

A garland of an intertwined rose, thistle, shamrock and leek, with the legend 'FID DEF' around the top and 'SIXPENCE · 19XX' around the bottom.

Edge: Milled

Years Produced: 1953 to 1967 for the business strike, plus proofs in the sets of 1953 and 1970.

Varieties:

There are major varieties for the business strikes in 1953, 1955, 1964 and 1965 plus each of the proof strikes in both 1953 and 1970. There are minor varieties for 1964.

1953 Business Strike Sixpence:

Major Varieties:

The 1953 sixpence has two obverses (obverse 1 and obverse 2) paired with a single reverse (reverse A), giving the die pairs 1+A and 2+A. These two obverses are only found on the 1953 sixpence. Both types are catalogued by Davies with numbers 2480 and 2481.

Obverses:

Obverse 1:

- The 'L' of 'ELIZABETH' points to a border bead.
- The 'I' of 'ELIZABETH' points to the right of a bead. Also described as pointing to a space.
- The second 'A' in 'GRATIA' points to the right of a bead.
- The 'MG' on the truncation is indistinct.
- The queen's silhouette is faint.
- The upright of the cross points to the right of a border bead.

Obverse 2:

- The 'L' of 'ELIZABETH' points to the right of a bead. Described by some as to a space between border beads.
- The 'I' of 'ELIZABETH' points to the left of a bead. Also described as to a space between beads
- The second 'A' in 'GRATIA' points to the left of a border bead. Described by some as to a border bead.
- The 'MG' on the truncation is clear.
- The queen's silhouette is sharper.
- The upright of the cross points to the left of a border bead.

Figure 132 – 1953 Sixpence Obverses (1)

Obverse 1	Obverse 2
'L' of 'ELIZABETH' to a bead	'L' of 'ELIZABETH' to right of bead
'I' of 'ELIZABETH' to right of bead	'I' of 'ELIZABETH' to left of bead.

120

Figure 133 – 1953 Sixpence Obverses (2)

Obverse 1
Second 'A' of 'GRATIA'
to right of bead

Obverse 2
Second 'A' of 'GRATIA'
to left of a bead

Figure 134 – 1953 Sixpence Obverses (3)

Obverse 1
Faint silhouette

Obverse 2
Sharper silhouette

Figure 135 – 1953 Sixpence Obverses (4)

Obverse 1
Cross to right of bead

Obverse 2
Cross to left of bead

The distinctness of the initials 'MG' on the truncation is very difficult to use as an identifier, except for high grade specimens and it is recommended that one of the above more readily identifiable characteristics is used as a positive identifier.

Minor Varieties:

For this date there are no reported minor varieties.

1953 Proof Strike Sixpence:

Major Varieties:

Similar to the business strike, there are two varieties of the proof sixpence, with two obverses (obverse 1 and obverse 2) and a single reverse (reverse A) giving die pairs 1+A and 2+A. These have the same identifiers as the business strike and are as illustrated in figures 132 - 135. They are catalogued by Davies as 2480 and 2481, as for the business strike, although the 1+A type is shown as unconfirmed.

Minor Varieties:

For this date and strike there are no reported minor varieties.

1955 Sixpence:

Major Varieties:

The 1955 sixpence has a single obverse (obverse 3) matched with two different reverses (reverse B and reverse C), giving the die pairs 1+B and 1+C. Reverse B is found on sixpences of 1954 and 1955, whilst reverse C is found on sixpences from 1955 through to 1964.

It should be noted that Davies catalogues the 1953 reverse A as being identical to the 1954 reverse A, whereas other sources describe differences between them and regard the reverse of the 1954 sixpence as reverse B. The result of this is that Davies catalogues the reverses for 1955 as reverses A and B, whilst others catalogue them as reverses B and C.

The differences between reverse A of 1953 and reverse B of 1954 are minute. For reverse A, the 'I' of 'SIXPENCE' points to the right of a border tooth, whilst for reverse B it points to a space between beads. Also, on reverse A, the upright of the 'F' in 'DEF' points to a space, whilst on reverse B, it points to a border bead.

Reverses:

Reverse B:

- The 'F' of 'FID' points to a border bead.
- The 'D' of 'FID' points to a border bead.
- The 'I' of 'FID' points to a border bead.
- The 'I' of 'SIXPENCE' points to a space between border beads.
- The border beads are thicker with a smaller space between them.

122

Reverse C:

- The 'F' of 'FID' points to a space between border beads.
- The 'D' of 'FID' points to a space.
- The 'I' of 'FID' points to a space.
- The 'I' of SIXPENCE' points slightly to the right of a border bead.
- The border beads are thinner with a wider gap between them.

Figure 136 – 1955 Sixpence Reverses (1)

Reverse B	Reverse C
The 'F' of 'FID' to a bead	The 'F' of 'FID' to a space
The 'I' of 'FID' to a bead	The 'I' of 'FID' to a space
The 'D' of 'FID' to a bead	The 'D' of 'FID' to a space
Thicker border beads	Thinner border beads
Smaller gap between beads	Wider gap between beads

Figure 137 – 1955 Sixpence Reverses (2)

Reverse B	Reverse C
The 'I' of 'SIX' to a space	The 'I' of 'SIX' to right of bead

Minor Varieties:

For this date there are no reported minor varieties.

1964 Sixpence:

Major Varieties:

The 1964 sixpence has two obverses (obverse 3 and obverse 4) and a single reverse (reverse C) giving the die pairs 3+C and 4+C. These are catalogued with numbers 2501 and 2502 by Davies. Because of the way in which Davies catalogues this series, these equate to the pairings 1+B and 2+B according to Davies. Of the two the 4+C pairing is scarcer.

Obverses:

Obverse 3:

- The second 'A' of 'GRATIA' points to a space between beads.
- The 'I' of 'REGINA' points to a space between border beads.
- Beads are close to the rim, but not touching it.
- The beads are slightly larger than on obverse 4.
- The portrait is normally engraved with no incuse eyebrow.
- It has 92 border beads.

Obverse 4:

- The second 'A' of 'GRATIA' points to a border bead.
- The 'I' of 'REGINA' points to a border bead.
- Beads are further away from the rim, than on obverse 3.
- The beads are slightly smaller than on obverse 3.
- The queen's portrait is slightly re-engraved with the eyebrow becoming an incuse line.
- There are 95 border teeth.

Figure 138 – 1964 Sixpence Obverses (1)

Obverse 3	**Obverse 4**
The second 'A' of 'GRATIA' to a space	The second 'A' of 'GRATIA' to a bead

Figure 139 – 1964 Sixpence Obverses (2)

Obverse 3	**Obverse 4**
The 'I' of 'REGINA' to a space Beads close to rim	The 'I' of 'REGINA' to a bead Beads away from the rim

Figure 140 – 1964 Sixpence Obverses (3)

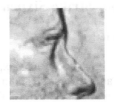

Obverse 3
No incuse eyebrow

Obverse 4
Incuse eyebrow

Counting the border teeth is not recommended as a first choice means of differentiating these two types.

Minor Varieties:

For 1964 sixpences, the Obverse 3 major variety is found as one of two minor types. Of these, the first type is scarcer than the second.

Obverse 3 Type 1:

- The bust is 12.5mm high.
- The border beads are away from the edge.
- Normal sized rim thickness.

Obverse 3 Type 2:

- The bust is 12.75mm high.
- The border beads touch the edge.
- A narrower rim.

Examples are also found with a missing 'I' in 'GRATIA' probably caused by a blocked die.

1965 Sixpence:

Major Varieties:

As for the 1964 sixpence, the 1965 also has the two obverses (obverse 3 and obverse 4) and a single reverse (but this time reverse D) giving the die pairs 3+D and 4+D, catalogued by Davies as 2503 and 2504. Again, because of the way in which Davies catalogues this series, these equate to the pairings 1+C and 2+C according to Davies. Of the two the 3+D pairing is very much scarcer.

The identifiers for the two obverses are the same as for 1964 and are as shown in figures 138 - 140.

1970 Proof Strike Sixpence:

Major Varieties:

As for the 1964 and 1965 sixpences, the 1970 proof strike has the two obverses (obverse 4 and obverse 5) and a single reverse (but this time reverse E) giving the die pairs 4+E and 5+E. As before, the way in which Davies catalogues this series, means that these equate to the pairings 2+D and 3+D. Of the two, the 3+D pairing is unconfirmed in Davies, although specimens have subsequently been confirmed to exist. Davies catalogues these two types with numbers 2507 and 2508.

Obverses:

Obverse 4:

- The second 'A' of 'GRATIA' points to a border bead.
- The 'I' of 'GRATIA' points to the right of a border bead.

Obverse 5:

- The second 'A' of 'GRATIA' points to the right of a border bead.
- The 'I' of 'GRATIA' points to a space.

Figure 141 – 1970 Proof Sixpence Obverses

Obverse 4	**Obverse 5**
The 'A' of 'GRATIA' to a bead	The 'A' of 'GRATIA' to right of a bead
The 'I' of 'GRATIA' to right of a bead	The 'I' of 'GRATIA' to a space

The Long Leek Variety:

The long leek variety arises, like the quatrefoil types of the English shillings, from a tendency for die cracks to appear, in this case from the tip of the leek to the rim beads of the coin. Long leek varieties are known for 1953 (2+A), 1954, 1955 (Rev B), 1956, 1957, 1958, 1959, 1962, 1963, 1964 (3+C, type 2) and 1966.

Filled Dies:

Elizabeth II sixpences seem to be affected by filled dies more than any of the other denominations of this reign. Examples exist as follows:

1. 1965 with the '5' and the 'CT' indistinct.
2. 1966 with the 'CT' missing.
3. 1967 with all the obverse lettering missing except the 'E' and 'A' in 'REGINA'.
4. 1967 with both obverse and reverse designs weak all over.

*   *   *   *   *

Denomination: Shilling

1953   1954 -1970

1953 – 1970
English   Scottish

Specification: Diameter: 24mm
Weight: 5.7g
Metal: Cupronickel: Copper 75%
Nickel 25%

Obverse Design:

Elizabeth's bust facing right with abbreviated legend as follows:

1. 'ELIZABETH II DEI GRATIA BRITT:OMN:REGINA +' – 1953 only
2. 'ELIZABETH · II · DEI · GRATIA · REGINA +' – 1954 to 1970

Reverse Design:

As for the George VI shilling series, each year in which shillings were produced has two basic reverse designs issued: an English shield and a Scottish shield.

1. For the English shield, three leopards within a crowned shield, which separates the date and the inscription 'FID DEF' round the top of the coin and 'ONE SHILLING' round the bottom.

2. For the Scottish shield, similar, but with a rampant lion within a crowned shield and the same legends.

Edge: Milled

Years Produced: 1953 to 1966 for both types, plus proofs in the sets of 1953 and 1970. Unusually, for this reign, there were no shillings of either type dated 1967 just prior to decimalisation.

Varieties:

There are major varieties for the business strikes with the English reverse in 1953 and 1956, plus the proof for 1953. For the Scottish shilling major varieties occur in 1953 and 1955 plus the proof strikes for 1953. There are also minor varieties for the years 1955 (both English and Scottish types), 1959 (Scottish), 1963 (Scottish) and 1966 (Scottish).

1953 Business Strike English Shilling:

Major Varieties:

The 1953 English shilling has two obverses (obverse 1 and obverse 2) paired with a single reverse (reverse A), giving the die pairs 1+A and 2+A. These two obverses are only found on the 1953 shilling and are catalogued by Davies as 2400 and 2401.

Obverses:

Obverse 1:

- The 'I' of 'ELIZABETH' points to a border bead.
- The 'I' in 'GRATIA' points to a space between border beads.
- 'MG' on the truncation is indistinct.
- The queen's silhouette is faint and slightly smaller.
- The colon after 'OMN' points to a space.
- The legs of the 'N' of 'OMN' point to border beads.
- The truncation is further from the 'R' in 'BRITT'.

Obverse 2:

- The 'I' of 'ELIZABETH' points to a space between border beads.
- The 'I' in 'GRATIA' points to the right of a border bead. Some sources quote this as being to a bead.
- 'MG' on the truncation is clear.
- The queen's silhouette is sharper and larger than on obverse 1.
- The colon after 'OMN' points to a border bead.
- The legs of the 'N' of 'OMN' point to spaces between border beads.
- The truncation is closer to the 'R' in 'BRITT'.

Figure 142 – 1953 English Shilling Obverses (1)

Obverse 1
The 'I' of 'ELIZABETH'
points to a bead

Obverse 2
The 'I' of 'ELIZABETH'
points to a space

Figure 143 – 1953 English Shilling Obverses (2)

Obverse 1
The 'I' of 'GRATIA'
points to a space

Obverse 2
The 'I' of 'GRATIA'
points to right of a bead

Figure 144 – 1953 English Shilling Obverses (3)

Obverse 1
Faint Effigy
Indistinct 'MG'

Obverse 2
Sharper effigy
Distinct 'MG'

Figure 145 – 1953 English Shilling Obverses (4)

Obverse 1
Colon to a space
Legs of the 'N' to beads

Obverse 2
Colon to a bead
Legs of the 'N' to spaces

130

Figure 146 – 1953 English Shilling Obverses (5)

Obverse 1
'R' away from truncation

Obverse 2
'R' close to truncation

As for the sixpence, the distinctness of the 'MG' initials on the truncation is not the best identifier for the two types.

Minor Varieties:

There are no reported minor varieties for the 1953 English shilling. However, there is an error type coin, where the obverse was struck on both sides. The date is identifiable for this type from the legend which is unique to 1953 only. These errors are extremely rare.

1953 Proof Strike English Shilling:

Major Varieties:

The proof English shilling as found in the 1953 proof sets, like the business strike, also has two obverses (obverse 1 and obverse 2) paired with a single reverse (reverse A), giving the die pairs 1+A and 2+A. These are numbered 2400 and 2401 by Davies. Of these, the 1+A variety is recorded as unconfirmed by Davies.

The identifiers for the proof English shilling varieties are identical to those for the business strike and are as shown in figures 142 – 146.

Minor Varieties:

There are no reported minor varieties for the 1953 English proof shilling.

1953 Business Strike Scottish Shilling:

Major Varieties:

Apart from the shield design, the 1953 Scottish shilling is identical to the English version and has two obverses (obverse 1 and obverse 2) paired with a single reverse (reverse A), giving the die pairs 1+A and 2+A. These two types are numbered 2440 and 2441 by Davies. Again, these are only found on the 1953 shilling. The identifiers for the Scottish shilling varieties are identical to those for the 1953 English type and are as shown in figures 142 – 146.

Minor Varieties:

There are no reported minor varieties for the 1953 English shilling.

1953 Proof Strike Scottish Shilling:

Major Varieties:

The proof Scottish shilling as found in the 1953 proof sets also has two obverses (obverse 1 and obverse 2) paired with a single reverse (reverse A), giving the die pairs 1+A and 2+A. Like the English proof shilling, the 1+A variety is recorded as unconfirmed by Davies, although examples have been subsequently found. These two types are numbered 2440 and 2441 by Davies.

The identifiers for the proof Scottish shilling varieties are identical to those for the business strike plus the English business and proof strikes and are as shown in figures 142 – 146.

Minor Varieties:

There are no reported minor varieties for the 1953 Scottish proof shilling.

1955 English Shilling:

Major Varieties:

The 1955 English shilling has a single obverse (obverse 3) paired with a single reverse (reverse C), giving the simple die pair 3+C and, hence, no major varieties. As in the case of the sixpence, the obverse and reverse numbering of Davies differs from that of other cataloguers. The die pair 3+C referred to here, corresponds to 1+B according to Davies.

Minor Varieties:

There are two minor varieties of the 1955 English shilling. The most common type has the normal sized reverse design and edge thickness and is numbered 2411 by Davies. The scarcer type has a smaller design, defined by Davies as 19.5mm with number 2412, and a thicker reverse edge.

Differentiating these by the design size is very difficult for the naked eye, but can be achieved by enlarging suitable photographs of each type. However, there are several other more definitive indicators for the two types:

Reverse C Type 1:

- The edge rim is thinner
- Small gap between the shield and legend.
- Normal sized design, with a wider gap between the 'O' and the 'G'.

Reverse C Type 2:

- The edge rim is thicker.
- Wider gap between the shield and legend.
- A smaller design with a narrower gap between the 'O' and the 'G'.

Figure 147 – 1955 English Shilling Reverses (1)

Normal Reverse C	**Smaller Reverse C**
Narrower edge rim	Wider edge rim

Figure 148 – 1955 English Shilling Reverses (2)

Normal Reverse C	**Smaller Reverse C**
Narrow gap shield to legend	Wider gap shield to legend

Some sources also claim that the smaller design has a larger gap between the top of the crown and the legend, but it has not proved possible to verify this with certainty.

1955 Scottish Shilling:

Major Varieties:

Like the 1955 English shilling, the Scottish shilling of this date has a single obverse (obverse 3) paired with reverse C, giving the die pair 3+C, but also has a major variety where obverse 3 is paired with a new reverse (reverse D). Davies numbers these as 2451 and 2453. As for the 1955 English shilling, the obverse and reverse numbering of Davies differs from that of other cataloguers. The die pairs 3+C and 3+D referred to here, correspond to 1+B and 1+C according to Davies.

Reverses:

Reverse C:

- The 'D' of 'DEF' points to a border bead.
- The 'F' of 'DEF' points to a space between border beads.
- The left quatrefoil points to a space.

133

- The right quatrefoil points to a space.
- The second 'I' in 'SHILLING' points to a border bead.
- There are 118 border beads.

Reverse D:

- The 'D' of 'DEF' points to a space.
- The 'F' of 'DEF' points to left of a bead.
- The left quatrefoil points to a border bead.
- The right quatrefoil points to the left of a bead.
- The second 'I' in 'SHILLING' points to a space between border beads.
- There are 119 border beads.

Figure 149 – 1955 Scottish Shilling Reverses (1)

Reverse C	**Reverse D**
'D' of 'DEF' to a bead	'D' of 'DEF' to a space
'F' of 'DEF' to a space	'F' of 'DEF' to left of a bead

Figure 150 – 1955 Scottish Shilling Reverses (2)

Reverse C	**Reverse D**
Left quatrefoil to a space	Left quatrefoil to a bead

Figure 151 – 1955 Scottish Shilling Reverses (3)

Reverse C	**Reverse D**
Right quatrefoil to a space	Right quatrefoil to left of bead

Figure 152 – 1955 Scottish Shilling Reverses (4)

Reverse C	**Reverse D**
Second 'I' in	Second 'I' in
'SHILLING' to bead	'SHILLING' to a space

As before, counting border teeth is not a recommended way to distinguish the two types.

Minor Varieties:

Like the English 1955 shilling, there are two minor varieties of the 1955 Scottish shilling with reverse C. The most common type has the normal sized design and edge thickness. The scarcer type has a smaller design, defined by Davies as 19.5mm, and with a thicker reverse edge. Davies catalogues this as number 2452.

Differentiating these by the design size is very difficult for the naked eye, but can be achieved by enlarging suitable photographs of each type. However, the edge thickness is a more readily identifiable means of distinguishing them. The difference is illustrated in figure 147, shown earlier for the English shilling of the same date.

1956 English Shilling:

Major Varieties:

For 1956, the English shilling has a single obverse (obverse 3) paired with two reverses (reverse C and reverse D) giving the dies pair 3+C and 3+D. As for earlier shillings, the obverse and reverse numbering of Davies differs from that of other cataloguers. The die pairs 3+C and 3+D referred to here, correspond to 1+B and 1+C according to Davies, and are numbered 2413 and 2414. Even allowing for the different shields, the designs of the English reverses C and D do not correspond with the designs for the Scottish reverses of the same designation.

Reverses:

Reverse C:

- The 'D' of 'FID' points to a space between border beads.
- The 'I' of 'FID' points to a border bead.
- The 'D' of 'DEF' points to a border bead.
- The right quatrefoil points to a border bead.
- It has a larger shield.

- There are 119 border beads.
- Normal sized design, with a wider gap between the 'O' and the 'G'.

Reverse D:

- The 'D' of 'FID' points to a border bead.
- The 'I' of 'FID' points to a space between border beads.
- The 'D' of 'DEF' points to left of a bead.
- The right quatrefoil points to the right of a border bead.
- It has a smaller shield.
- There are 118 border beads.
- A smaller sized design, with a narrower gap between the 'O' and the 'G'.

Counting border beads, measuring the size of the shield or the gap between the 'O' and the 'G' are not recommended as the best means of differentiating these two types.

Figure 153 – 1956 English Shilling Reverses (1)

Reverse C	**Reverse D**
The 'D' of 'FID' to a space	The 'D' of 'FID' to a bead
The 'I' of 'FID' to a bead	The 'I' of 'FID' to a space

Figure 154 – 1956 English Shilling Reverses (2)

Reverse C	**Reverse D**
The 'D' of 'DEF' to a bead	The 'D' of 'DEF' to left of a bead

Figure 155 – 1956 English Shilling Reverses (3)

Reverse C
Right quatrefoil to a bead

Reverse D
Right quatrefoil to right of bead

Minor Varieties:

There are no reported minor varieties for the 1956 English shilling.

1959 Scottish Shilling:

Major Varieties:

There are no reported major varieties for the 1959 Scottish shilling.

Minor Varieties:

The series of dates from 1956 to 1966 all have reverse D. However, for 1959 examples, reverse D is found as one two minor types.

Reverse D Type 1: This has the three diamond shaped ornaments at the base of the crown all touching the baseline.
Reverse D Type 2: This type has the centre and right hand diamond shaped ornaments clear of the baseline. The ornaments are less bulky than on the type 1 reverse.

The type 2 reverse appears to be the standard type found on all the other dates in the series.

Figure 156 – 1959 Scottish Shilling Reverses (1)

Reverse D Type 1
Ornaments on baseline
Larger ornaments

Reverse D Type 2
Centre and right away from baseline
Smaller ornaments

137

1963 Scottish Shilling:

Major Varieties:

There are no reported major varieties for the 1963 Scottish shilling.

Minor Varieties:

As for 1959, the 1963 Scottish shilling was struck with the major variety reverse D, again being found as one of two minor reverse varieties:

Reverse D Type 1:

- This has the three diamond shaped ornaments at the base of the crown all touching the baseline.
- The ornaments are bulkier than type 2.
- The lion's tongue has a shorter tip.
- No incuse lines in the lion's tail.

Reverse D Type 2:

- This type has the centre and right hand diamond shaped ornaments clear of the baseline.
- The ornaments are less bulky than on the type 1 reverse.
- The lion's tongue is slightly longer.
- There are incuse lines in the lion's tail.

Details of the crown ornaments are shown above in figure 156 for the 1959 Scottish shilling.

Figure 157 – 1963 Scottish Shilling Reverses (2)

Reverse D Type 1
Shorter tip of tongue
No incuse lines on rear tail

Reverse D Type 2
Longer tip of tongue
Incuse lines on rear tail

1966 Scottish Shilling:

There are no specific design varieties for the 1966 Scottish shilling. However, there are a few examples known where the obverse/reverse alignment differs from the standard coin. The usual arrangement is with the obverse and reverse upright in relation to each other i.e. where the coin is held between the fingers with the queen's head upright, and is spun through 180 degrees, the reverse is upright also.

The error variety for this date has the reverse upside down in relation to the obverse, when rotated in this way.

Cracked Quatrefoils:

On Elizabeth II shillings, the quatrefoil is the cross shaped ornament on either side of the shield. These are a particularly weak part of the reverse die, with die cracks affecting specimens of the English shilling series. Scottish shillings are not affected by this problem, due to the slightly different design shape of the quatrefoil on these coins. The die cracks are often accompanied by others especially through the letters in 'FID'.

Cracked quatrefoils occur either singly on either side or to both sides on the same coin and are scarce, but found on all dates from 1953 through to 1966. However, not all dates have all three types.

Diamond Shaped Crown Ornaments:

Earlier mention has been made of the size and alignment of the diamond shaped ornaments to the crown for the Scottish shilling of 1959. This type is a specific minor variety for this year. Many other years in this series also show a tendency for variations in the placing of the diamonds.

The left hand diamond is virtually always found in contact with the base line of the crown or only just clear, whilst the central diamond can be found in one of three positions:

1. Touching the base line of the crown.
2. Nearly touching the base line.
3. Well clear of the base line.

When well clear of the base line, the right hand diamond is also generally affected, being either just clear or well clear of the baseline.

No definitive study appears to have been carried out on this series to determine which combinations exist for both the English ands Scottish types, although variants are confirmed to exist for 1955, 1958, 1959, 1963 and 1965.

*   *   *   *   *

139

Denomination: Florin

1953   1954 - 1970

1953 – 1970

Specification: Diameter: 28.5mm
                     Weight: 11.3g
                     Metal: Cupronickel: Copper 75%
                                     Nickel 25%

Obverse Design:

Elizabeth's bust facing right with abbreviated legend as follows:

1. 'ELIZABETH II DEI GRATIA BRITT:OMN:REGINA +' – 1953 only
2. 'ELIZABETH · II · DEI · GRATIA · REGINA +' – 1954 to 1970

Reverse Design:

Concentric roses in the centre of the coin inside a ring of connected shamrocks, thistles and leeks. The inscription 'FID: DEF:' and the date around the top. The words 'TWO SHILLINGS' plus the date around the lower half.

Edge: Milled.

Years Produced: 1953 to 1967, plus proofs in the sets of 1953 and 1970.

Varieties:

For this date run there is a major variety of the business strike of 1953 only and for the proof strikes of 1953 and 1970. There is also a minor variety for the 1953 business coin and for 1965 and 1966, plus error types for 1962 and 1967.

140

1953 Business Strike Florin:

Major Varieties:

The business strike florin of 1953 has two obverses (obverse 1 and obverse 2) and a single reverse (reverse A) giving the varieties 1+A and 2+A and numbered 2360 and 2361 by Davies. These two obverses are only found on the 1953 shilling.

Obverse 1:

- The 'I' of 'ELIZABETH' points to a space.
- A faint silhouette.
- The 'I' of 'DEI' points to a border bead. More correctly, this is slightly to the right of a bead.
- The upright of the 'B' in 'BRITT' points to a space between border beads.

Obverse 2:

- The 'I' of 'ELIZABETH' points to a border bead.
- A sharper silhouette.
- The 'I' of 'DEI' points to a space between beads.
- The upright of the 'B' in 'BRITT' points to the right of a border bead.

Figure 158 – 1953 Florin Obverses (1)

Obverse A	**Obverse B**
'I' of 'ELIZABETH'	'I' of 'ELIZABETH'
to a space	to a bead

Figure 159 – 1953 Florin Obverses (2)

Obverse 1	**Obverse 2**
Faint Effigy	Sharper effigy

Figure 160 – 1953 Florin Obverses (3)

Obverse 1   **Obverse 2**
The 'I' of 'DEI to a bead   The 'I' of 'DEI' to a space

Figure 161 – 1953 Florin Obverses (4)

Obverse 1   **Obverse 2**
The 'B' of 'BRITT to a space   The 'B' of 'BRITT' to right of bead

Minor Varieties:

For obverse 1, there are two minor varieties.

Obverse 1 Type 1: The 'MG' on the truncation is indistinct.
Obverse 1 Type 2: The 'MG' on the truncation is sharp as on obverse 2.

1953 Proof Strike Florin:

Major Varieties:

Like the business strike, the proof strike 1953 florin as found in the proof sets also has two obverses (obverse 1 and obverse 2) paired with a single reverse (reverse A), giving the die pairs 1+A and 2+A and numbered as for the business strike. Of these, the 1+A variety is recorded as unconfirmed by Davies.

The identifiers for the proof florin varieties are identical to those for the business strike and are as shown in figures 158 - 161.

Minor Varieties:

There are no reported minor varieties for the 1953 proof florin

1962 Florin:

Major Varieties:

There are no reported major design varieties for the 1962 florin.

Minor Varieties:

There are no reported minor design varieties for the 1962 florin. However, due to a blocked die, there are specimens known where the 'O' of 'TWO' and the 'SHI' of 'SHILLINGS' are both missing.

1965 Florin:

Major Varieties:

There are no reported major design varieties for the 1965 florin.

Minor Varieties:

There are no reported minor design varieties for the 1965 florin. However, specimens exist with a doubled date and legend.

1966 Florin:

Major Varieties:

There are no reported major design varieties for the 1966 florin.

Minor Varieties:

There are no reported minor design varieties for the 1966 florin. However, many specimens exhibit a doubling of the border beads on the obverse, which has not arisen through double striking.

Also, like the 1965 florin, there are specimens found with a doubled date and legend.

1967 Florin:

Major Varieties:

There are no reported major design varieties for the 1967 florin.

Minor Varieties:

There are no reported minor varieties for the 1967 florin. However, there is a rare error type coin, where the reverse was struck on both sides. Also, like the 1965 and 1966 florins, there are specimens found with a doubled date and legend.

1970 Proof Strike Florin:

Major Varieties:

As for the 1970 sixpence, the 1970 florin proof strike has two obverses (obverse 3 and obverse 4) and a single reverse (reverse C) giving the die pairs 3+C and 4+C. As before, the way in which Davies catalogues this series, means that these equate to the pairings 1+B and 2+B. Of the two, the 3+C pairing is unconfirmed in Davies, although specimens have subsequently been confirmed to exist. They are numbered 2384 an 2385 respectively by Davies.

Obverses:

Obverse 3:

- The second 'A' of 'GRATIA' points to a space between border beads.
- The 'E' of 'DEI' points to a space between border beads.
- The 'I' of 'ELIZABETH' points to left of a bead.

Obverse 4:

- The second 'A' of 'GRATIA' points to a border bead.
- The 'E' of 'DEI' points to a border bead.
- The 'I' of 'ELIZABETH' points to the right of a bead.

Figure 162 – 1970 Proof Florin Obverses (1)

Obverse 3	**Obverse 4**
The second 'A' of	The second 'A' of
'GRATIA' to a space	'GRATIA' to a bead

Figure 163 – 1970 Proof Florin Obverses (2)

Obverse 3	**Obverse 4**
The 'E' of 'DEI'	The 'E' of 'DEI'
to a space	to a bead

Figure 164 – 1970 Proof Florin Obverses (3)

Obverse 3
The 'I' of 'ELIZ'
to left of bead

Obverse 4
The 'I' of 'ELIZ'
to right of a bead

Minor Varieties:

There are no reported minor varieties for the 1970 florin

*   *   *   *   *

Denomination: Halfcrown

1953   1954 - 1970

1953 – 1970

Specification: Diameter: 32mm
Weight: 14.1g
Metal: Cupronickel: Copper 75%
                      Nickel 25%

Obverse Design:

Elizabeth's bust facing right with abbreviated legend as follows:

1. 'ELIZABETH II DEI GRATIA BRITT:OMN:REGINA +' – 1953 only
2. 'ELIZABETH · II · DEI · GRATIA · REGINA +' – 1954 to 1970

Reverse Design:

A crowned shield, flanked by the letters 'E' and 'R' and with 'FID· ·DEF' around the top and the words 'HALF CROWN 19XX' around the bottom.

Edge: Milled.

Years Produced: 1953 to 1967, plus proofs in the sets of 1953 and 1970.

Varieties:

For this date run there are major varieties of the business strike for 1953, 1961 and 1962 and also for both of the proof strikes of 1953 and 1970. There is also a minor design variety for 1953 and for 1961, in the latter case caused by a blocked die.

146

1953 Business Strike Halfcrown:

Major Varieties:

The business strike halfcrown of 1953 has two obverses (obverse 1 and obverse 2) and a single reverse (reverse A) giving the varieties 1+A and 2+A. Davies catalogues them with numbers 2310 and 2311. These two obverses are only found on the 1953 shilling. Of these, the 2+A is most common.

Obverses:

Obverse 1:

- The 'I' of 'DEI' points to a space between border beads.
- The first 'A' of 'GRATIA' points to a space between border beads.
- The 'I' of 'ELIZABETH' to a space.
- Faint silhouette.
- There are 123 border beads.

Obverse 2:

- The 'I' of 'DEI' points to a border bead.
- The first 'A' of 'GRATIA' points to a border bead.
- The 'I' of 'ELIZABETH' to right of a border bead.
- Clear silhouette.
- There are 127 border beads.

Figure 165 – 1953 Business Halfcrown Obverses (1)

| **Obverse 1** | **Obverse 2** |
| The 'I' of 'DEI' to a space | The 'I' of 'DEI' to a bead |

Figure 166 – 1953 Business Halfcrown Obverses (2)

| **Obverse 1** | **Obverse 2** |
| 1st 'A' of 'GRATIA' to space | 1st 'A' of 'GRATIA' to bead |

147

The faint and distinct effigies are illustrated in figures 144 (English shilling) and 159 florin and are not repeated here.

Figure 167 – 1953 Business Halfcrown Obverses (3)

Obverse 1	**Obverse 2**
The 'I' of 'ELIZ' to a space	The 'I' of 'ELIZ' to right of bead

Minor Varieties:

For obverse 1, like the 1953 florin, there are two minor varieties, both of which are about equal in scarcity.

Obverse 1 Type 1: The 'MG' on the truncation is indistinct.
Obverse 2 Type 2: The 'MG' on the truncation is sharp as on obverse 2.

1953 Proof Strike Halfcrown:

Major Varieties:

Like the business strike, the proof strike 1953 halfcrown is found in the proof sets and also has two obverses (obverse 1 and obverse 2) paired with a single reverse (reverse A), giving the die pairs 1+A and 2+A and numbered by Davies as for the business strike. Of these, the 1+A variety is recorded as unconfirmed by Davies.

The identifiers for the proof halfcrown varieties are identical to those for the business strike and are as shown in figures 165 – 167.

Minor Varieties:

There are no reported minor varieties for the 1953 proof halfcrown.

1961 Halfcrown

Major Varieties:

Unusually, the 1961 halfcrown has two major varieties, based not on the obverse or reverse designs, but on the quality of the struck blanks. The 1961 coins are found either with the normal rather dull finish or with a bright almost proof-like finish, the latter being the scarcer type. Davies catalogues these as 2327 and 2328 respectively. The reasons for this strike are not known for certain, although it is clear that there are no good historical or celebratory reasons for a proof-like finish in this year.

The proof-like coins are sometimes referred to as having been struck from a polished die. However, it has been suggested that the die used was a normal business strike die but that the blanks used for this strike were leftovers from the 1953 proof strike, in which case they should be more properly referred to as polished flan types.

The differences between the two types are not easy to see from photographs but are very obvious in the hand.

Minor Varieties:

There is also a minor variety for the 1961 halfcrown, where the small initials 'E F' underneath the shield are missing, due to a blocked die, giving two types of 1961 halfcrown.

Reverse C Type 1: EF Present
Reverse C Type 2: EF Missing

Figure 168 – 1961 Halfcrown Reverses

ReverseC1
Normal EF

Reverse C2
EF Missing

1962 Halfcrown:

Major Varieties:

The halfcrown of 1962 has two obverses (obverse 3 and obverse 4) and two reverses (reverse C and reverse D) giving the varieties 3+C, 3+D, 4+C and 4+D, an arrangement known as a 'crossover mule'. As for the lower denominations of the Elizabeth II 'silver' coinage, the Davies numbering is different and catalogues these four types as 1+B, 1+C, 2+B, and 2+C, with the numbers 2329, 2330, 2331 and 2332. Of the four types, the 3+C and 4+D are most common, whilst the 3+D and 4+C are scarce.

Obverses:

Obverse 3:

- The 'I' of 'GRATIA' points to a space between border beads.
- The portrait is normally engraved with no incuse eyebrow.

149

- The 'I' of 'DEI' points to the left of a bead.
- There are 122 border beads.

Obverse 4:

- The 'I' of 'GRATIA' points to a border bead.
- The queen's portrait is slightly re-engraved with the eyebrow becoming an incuse line.
- The 'I' of 'DEI' points to a space.
- There are 124 border beads.

Figure 169 – 1962 Business Halfcrown Obverses (1)

Obverse 3	**Obverse 4**
The 'I' of	The 'I' of
'GRATIA' to a space	'GRATIA' to a bead

Figure 170 – 1962 Business Halfcrown Obverses (2)

Obverse 3	**Obverse 4**
Plain eyebrow	Incuse eyebrow

Figure 171 – 1962 Business Halfcrown Obverses (3)

Obverse 3	**Obverse 4**
'I' of 'DEI' to left of bead	'I' of 'DEI' to a space

Reverses:

Reverse C:

- The 'D' of 'DEF' points to a border bead.
- The rim is of medium thickness.
- The left limb of the 'N' in 'CROWN' points to a border bead.
- The border beads are smaller with wider gaps.
- The right-hand cross points to a space between border beads.
- The last bead on the right arch of the crown is partly obscured by the cross.
- The left leg of the 'A' in 'HALF' points to a space.
- There are 132 border beads.

Reverse D:

- The 'D' of 'DEF' points to a space between border beads.
- The rim is narrower.
- The left limb of the 'N' in 'CROWN' points to a space between border beads.
- The border beads are larger with narrower gaps.
- The right-hand cross points to a border bead.
- The last bead on the right arch of the crown is clear of the cross.
- The left leg of the 'A' in 'HALF' points to left of a border bead.
- There are 134 border beads.

Figure 172 – 1962 Business Halfcrown Reverses (1)

Reverse C	**Reverse D**
'D' of 'DEF' to bead	'D' of 'DEF' to space
Medium rim	Thinner rim

Figure 173 – 1962 Business Halfcrown Reverses (2)

Reverse C	**Reverse D**
Left leg of 'N' in 'CROWN' to a bead. Larger gap between beads Smaller beads	Left leg of 'N' in 'CROWN' to a space Smaller gap between beads Larger beads

Figure 174 – 1962 Business Halfcrown Reverses (3)

Reverse C	**Reverse D**
Cross points to a space Smaller beads	Cross points to a bead Larger beads

Figure 175 – 1962 Business Halfcrown Reverses (4)

Reverse C	**Reverse D**
Bead partially obscured	Bead clear

Figure 176 – 1962 Business Halfcrown Reverses (5)

Reverse C	**Reverse D**
Left leg of 'A' to a space	Left leg of 'A' to left of a bead

Minor Varieties:

There are no reported minor varieties for the 1962 halfcrown.

1970 Proof Strike Halfcrown:

Major Varieties:

As for the lower denomination 'silver' coins, the 1970 halfcrown proof strike has two obverses (obverse 4 and obverse 5) and a single reverse (reverse D) giving the die pairs 4+D and 5+D. As before, the way in which Davies catalogues this series, means that these equate to the pairings 2+C and 3+C, which are catalogued with numbers 2338 and 2339. Of the two, the 4+D pairing is unconfirmed in Davies, although specimens have subsequently been confirmed to exist.

Obverses:

Obverse 4:

- The 'I' of 'GRATIA' points to a border bead.
- The leg of 'B' in 'ELIZABETH' points to a space.

Obverse 5:

- The 'I' of 'GRATIA' points to the right of a border bead.
- The leg of 'B' in 'ELIZABETH' points to a border bead.

Figure 177 – 1970 Proof Halfcrown Obverses (1)

Obverse 4
The 'I' of
'GRATIA' to a bead

Obverse 5
The 'I' of
'GRATIA' to right of bead

Figure 178 – 1970 Proof Halfcrown Obverses (2)

Obverse 4
The 'B' of
'ELIZABETH' to a space

Obverse 5
The 'B' of
'ELIZABETH' to a bead

Minor Varieties:

There are no reported minor varieties for the 1970 halfcrown.

*　　*　　*　　*　　*

154

Denomination: Crown

1953

1960

1965

Specification: Diameter: 39mm
                      Weight: 28.3g
                      Metal: Cupronickel: Copper 75%
                                       Nickel 25%

Obverse Designs:

Each of the crowns of Elizabeth's reign is unique and they don't form any kind of consistent series.

1. For 1953, Elizabeth is seated on a horse and facing front left with abbreviated legend as follows:

'ELIZABETH · II · DEI · GRATIA · BRITT OMN · REGINA · FIDEI · DEFENSOR FIVE SHILLINGS'

2. For 1960, the queen's head facing right with the legend: 'ELIZABETH II DEI GRATIA REGINA F·D· FIVE SHILLINGS'

3. For 1965, the queen's head facing right with the legend: 'ELIZABETH II DEI GRATIA REGINA F·D· 1965'

Reverse Designs:

1. For 1953 and 1960, a cruciform of shields with national emblems in the spaces, all around a crown, and with the date on either side of the leek.

2. For 1965 the bust of Sir Winston Churchill with the single word 'CHURCHILL' around the right hand side of the coin.

Edge:

1. 1953: The incuse inscription 'FAITH AND TRUTH I WILL BEAR UNTO YOU'. This inscription may be either way up on the edge.

2. 1960 and 65 - milled

Years Produced: 1953, 1960 and 1965 plus a proof for 1953 from the set.

Varieties:

For this denomination there are major varieties for each date of business strike and for the 1953 proof strike. There are also minor varieties for the 1953, 1960 and 1965 business strikes.

1953 Business Strike Crown:

Major Varieties:

The business strike crown of 1953 is found with one of two obverse types (obverse 1 and obverse 2) and paired with a single reverse (reverse A) to give the pairings 1+A and 2+A. Davies catalogues these with numbers 2280 and 2281.

Obverse 1:

- The 'I' of 'GRATIA' points to a border bead.
- Larger loop 'R's in the monograms.
- The 'II' inside the right hand monogram is taller.
- There are 114 beads of both sizes.

Obverse 2:

- The 'I' of 'GRATIA' points to a space between border beads (more correctly to a smaller border bead).
- Smaller loop 'R's in the monograms.
- The 'II' inside the right hand monogram is shorter.
- There are 112 beads of both sizes.

Figure 179 – 1953 Business Strike Crown Obverses (1)

Obverse 1	**Obverse 2**
The 'I' of	The 'I' of
'GRATIA' to a bead	'GRATIA' to a space.

Figure 180 – 1953 Business Strike Crown Obverses (2)

Obverse 1	**Obverse 2**
Larger loop to the 'R'	Small loop to the 'R'
Taller 'II'	Shorter 'II'

Minor Varieties:

A few coins were struck in error, where the edge inscription reads 'FAITH AND TRUTH I WILL BEAR UNTO YO,' missing out the 'U' on the end.

1953 Proof Strike Crown:

Major Varieties:

Like the business strike, the proof strike 1953 crown, as found in the proof sets, also has two obverses (obverse 1 and obverse 2) paired with a single reverse (reverse A), giving the die pairs 1+A and 2+A. Of these, the 2+A variety is recorded as unconfirmed by Davies. Davies catalogues these with the same numbers as the business strikes above. The identifiers for the proof crown varieties are identical to those for the business strike and are as shown in figures 179 and 180.

Minor Varieties:

There are no reported minor varieties for the 1953 proof strike crown.

1960 Crown:

Major Varieties:

Like the 1961 halfcrown, the 1960 crown has two major varieties, based not on the obverse or reverse designs, but on the quality of the strike. The finish is either the standard business strike or a proof-like type, struck for the British Trade Fair in New York, which used a specially polished die. The polished die version is scarce compared to the standard strike.

The differences between the two types are not easy to see from photographs but are very obvious in the hand.

Minor Varieties:

There are two types of the 1960 polished die crown:

Type 1: A narrowly spaced '60' in the date, with the '0' away from the shield.
Type 2: A more widely spaced '60' in the date, with the '0' closer to the shield.

Figure 181 – 1960 Polished Die Crown Reverses

Type 1	**Type 2**
Narrow '60'	Wider '60'
'0' away from shield	'0 closer to shield

These probably arose through the use of a dateless working punch left over from 1953.

There are also specimens of this date found without edge milling. These appear to have been struck unintentionally.

1965 Crown:

Major Varieties:

The 1965 Churchill crown has a single obverse type (obverse 1) paired with one of two reverses (reverse A and reverse B), giving the die pairs 1+A and 1+B. Davies numbers these two types as 2300 and 2301.

Reverse A:

- The 'C' and 'H' in 'CHURCHILL' are thicker.
- The edge decoration consists of linked smooth semi-circles with sharper points.
- Smaller external loop to the 'R' in 'CHURCHILL'.
- A larger internal loop to the 'R'.

Reverse B:

- The 'C' and 'H' in 'CHURCHILL' are thinner.
- The edge decoration consists of linked angular semi-circles with thicker points.
- Larger external loop to the 'R' in 'CHURCHILL'.
- A smaller internal loop to the 'R'.

Figure 182 – 1965 Crown Reverses (1)

Reverse A	Reverse B
Thicker 'C' and 'H'	Thinner 'C' and 'H'
Circular edge decoration	Angular edge decoration
Sharper points	Thicker points

Figure 183 – 1965 Crown Reverses (2)

Reverse A	Reverse B
Smaller loop to the 'R'	Larger loop to the 'R'
Larger internal loop to the 'R'	Smaller internal loop to the 'R'

Minor Varieties:

For coins with reverse B, there is a rare minor variety where the coin has a plain edge instead of being milled.

*   *   *   *   *

DECIMAL COINAGE

Elizabeth II

Period 1971 - 1999

Denomination: Five Pence

| 1968 – 1984 | 1985 – 1990 | 1990 – 1997 | 1998 - 1999 |

| 1968 – 1981 | 1982 – 1990 | 1990 – 1999 |

Specification: Diameter: 24mm (1968 -1990)
Diameter: 18mm (1990 - 1999 and to date)
Weight: 5.65g (1968 - 1990)
Weight: 3.25g (1990 - 1999)
Metal: Cupro-nickel (75% Copper/25% Nickel)

Obverse Design:

Elizabeth's bust facing right with abbreviated legend as follows:

1. 'D·G·REG·F·D·(date) ELIZABETH·II' – 1968 to 1984
2. 'ELIZABETH II D·G·REG·F·D·(date)' – 1985 to 1990 (large design)
3. 'ELIZABETH II D·G·REG·F·D·(date)' – 1990 to 1999 (smaller design)

Reverse Design:

1. A crowned thistle with '5' below and the inscription 'NEW PENCE' around the top – 1968 – 1981(proof).

2. A crowned thistle with '5' below and the inscription 'FIVE PENCE' around the top – 1982 – 1999 (large and small designs and to date).

161

Edge: Milled.

Years Produced: For circulation, 1968 – 1971, then 1975, and 1977 – 1980 followed by 1987 – 1989 for the larger diameter coins. Through the 1990s, the smaller diameter coins were struck for business purposes on all dates between 1990 and 1999, except 1993. Coins were also struck for the 'Brilliant Uncirculated' sets which were produced in each year starting in 1982 and for the proof sets, which were struck for every date from 1971 to 1999. It should be noted that the proof strikes from 1971 to 1974 were actually struck later, all around 1975.

Varieties:

Major varieties exist for the business strikes of 1980 only, with varieties of proofs in 1972, 1973, 1974, 1975, 1976 and 1977, the latter from the proof sets. Minor varieties occur for the business strikes in the years 1968, 1971 and 1990. There are no minor varieties for the proof five pences.

Some of the descriptors used to differentiate the varieties are quite fine distinctions, particularly where they include the terms 'to the right' and 'slightly to the right' etc. These refer to the precise pointing of the letter and are defined by the following illustration:

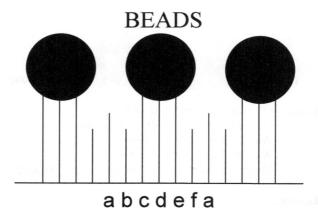

BEADS

a b c d e f a

a = to a space between beads.
b= to the left of a bead, or right of space.
c= slightly to the left of a bead.
d= to a bead.
e= slightly to the right of a bead.
f= to the right of a bead, or left of a space.

1968 Five Pence:

Major Varieties:

There are no major design varieties for the 1968 five pence.

Minor Varieties:

Although there are no specific design varieties for the 1968 five pence, there are several types found where a blocked die has caused the design not to be fully struck. Known types include:

- A missing '5'.
- Apparent changes to the queen's hairstyle.

1971 Business Strike Five Pence:

Major Varieties:

There are no major design varieties for the 1971 five pence.

Minor Varieties:

The 1971 business strike five pence has a single obverse (obverse 1) paired with a single reverse (reverse A) giving the die pair: 1+A. However, there is a minor variety of this single type, which can have either standard or broader edge milling. Davies identifies both types and catalogues them with numbers 2903 and 2904.

This very rare variety possibly arose from a rogue 'milling collar' and has 137 grooves as opposed to the usual 172 to 181 grooves for the normal types. It is not known if a study has been made of the number of milled grooves on these coins, but presumably if there are different numbers then these are all micro-varieties for this series, rather like the question of the numbers of nicks placed on the milling by the Royal Mint for the pre-decimal series of silver coins.

1972 Proof Strike Five Pence:

Major Varieties:

According to Davies, the 1972 proof strike five pence coin has a single obverse (obverse 1) coupled with a single reverse (reverse B) and is catalogued with number 2905. However, it has been subsequently found that there are two reverses found on this date, the earlier reverse A and the catalogued reverse B.

Reverses:

Reverse A:

- The 'P' of 'PENCE' points slightly left of a bead.
- The first 'E' of 'PENCE' points to slightly left of a bead.
- The first upright of the 'N' in 'PENCE' points slightly right of a bead.
- The second upright of the 'N' in 'PENCE' points slightly left of a bead.
- The second 'E' in 'PENCE' points to right of a bead.

163

- The first upright of the 'N' in 'NEW' points to slightly left of a bead.
- The second upright of the 'N' in 'NEW' points to slightly right of a bead.
- The 'E' of 'NEW' points to the left of a bead.
- There are small short serifs on the legend letters.
- The '5' is close to the border beads.
- There are 126 border beads.

Reverse B:

- The 'P' of 'PENCE' points the right of a bead.
- The first 'E' of 'PENCE' points to slightly right of a bead.
- The first upright of the 'N' in 'PENCE' points to a bead.
- The second upright of the 'N' in 'PENCE' points slightly right of a bead.
- The second 'E' in 'PENCE' points to a bead.
- The first upright of the 'N' in 'NEW' points to the right of a bead.
- The second upright of the 'N' in 'NEW' points to a bead.
- The 'E' of 'NEW' points to a space.
- There are large long serifs on the letters.
- The '5' is away from the border beads.
- There are 128 border beads.

Counting border beads is the least straightforward way to differentiate these two types, although it is a definitive one.

Figure 184 – 1972 Proof Five Pence Reverses (1)

Reverse A	**Reverse B**
'P' to slight left of bead	'P' to right of bead
1st 'E' points to left of bead	1st 'E' points to slightly right of bead
1st upright of 'N' to slightly right of bead	1st upright of 'N' to bead
2nd upright of 'N' to slightly left of bead	2nd upright of 'N' to right of bead
2nd 'E' points to right of bead	2nd 'E' points to bead

Figure 185 – 1972 Proof Five Pence Reverses (2)

Reverse A
1st upright of 'N' to left of bead
2nd upright of 'N' to right of bead
'E' points to left of bead
Small short serifs

Reverse B
1st upright of 'N' to right of bead
2nd upright of 'N' to a bead
'E' points to a space
Long large serifs

Figure 186 – 1972 Proof Five Pence Reverses (3)

Reverse A
'5' closer to border beads

Reverse B
'5' away from border beads

Minor Varieties:

There are no minor varieties for this date and denomination.

1973 Proof Strike Five Pence:

Major Varieties:

The 1973 proof strike five pence coin has, according to Davies, a single obverse (obverse 3) coupled with a single reverse (reverse B) and is catalogued with number 2906. However, as for 1972, it has been subsequently found that there are two reverses on this date, the earlier reverse A and the catalogued reverse B.

The differences are as described for the 1972 proof strike five pence and as illustrated in figures 184 – 186.

Minor Varieties:

There are no minor varieties for this date and denomination.

1974 Proof Strike Five Pence:

Major Varieties:

The 1974 proof strike five pence coin has, according to Davies, a single obverse (obverse 2) coupled with a single reverse (reverse B) and is catalogued with number 2907. However, as for 1972 and 1973, it has been subsequently found that there are two reverses for this date, the earlier reverse A and the catalogued reverse B.

The differences are as described for the 1972 proof strike five pence and as illustrated in figures 184 – 186.

Minor Varieties:

There are no minor varieties for this date and denomination.

1975 Proof Strike Five Pence:

Major Varieties:

As for earlier coins in the series, the proof strike five pence coin has, according to Davies, a single obverse (obverse 1) coupled with a single reverse (reverse B) and is catalogued with number 2909. However, as for 1972-74, it has since been found that there are two reverses for this date, the earlier reverse A and the catalogued reverse B.

The differences are as described for the 1972 proof strike five pence and as illustrated in figures 184 – 186.

Minor Varieties:

There are no minor varieties for this date and denomination.

1976 Proof Strike Five Pence:

Major Varieties:

As for 1974, the 1976 proof strike five pence coin has, according to Davies, a single obverse (obverse 2) coupled with a single reverse (reverse B) and is catalogued with number 2910. However, as for 1972-75, it has been subsequently found that there are two reverses for this date, the earlier reverse A and the catalogued reverse B.

The differences are as described for the 1972 proof strike five pence and as illustrated in figures 184 – 186.

Minor Varieties:

There are no minor varieties for this date and denomination.

1977 Proof Strike Five Pence:

The 1977 proof strike five pence is found with one of two obverse types (obverse 2 and obverse 4) paired to a single reverse (reverse B giving the die pairs: 2+B and 4+B. Davies catalogues these with numbers 2912 and 2913.

Obverse 2: Found also on the 1974 and 1976 proof strikes is characterised by:

- Hair outline is emphasised.
- The '1' of the date points to a bead.
- The border beads appear larger.
- The legend is closer to the border.

Obverse 4: Also found on the 1978 to 1980 proof strikes.

- Hair outline is less well defined.
- The '1' of the date points to a space.
- The border beads appear smaller.
- The legend is away from the border.

Figure 187 – 1977 Proof Five Pence Obverses (1)

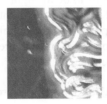

Obverse 2
Emphasised outline

Obverse 4
Less clear outline

Figure 188 – 1977 Proof Five Pence Obverses (2)

Obverse 2
'1' points to bead
Larger border beads
Legend closer to border

Obverse 4
'1' points to space
Smaller border beads
Legend away from border

Minor Varieties:

There are no minor design varieties for the 1977 five pence.

1980 Business Strike Five Pence:

The 1980 business strike five pence has a single obverse (obverse 4) paired with one of two reverses (reverse A and reverse B) giving the die pairs 4+A and 4+B. Davies catalogues these with the numbers 2918 and 2919. The 4+B types is scarcer than the 4+A.

Reverse A: As also found on the 1968 – 1979 business strikes.

- The left leg of the 'N' of 'NEW' points slightly to the left of a border bead.
- The right leg of the 'N' of 'NEW' points to a space between border beads. Considered by some to be slightly right of a bead.
- The 'E' of 'NEW' points to the left of a bead.
- The 'P' of 'PENCE' points to slightly left of a bead.
- The first 'E' of 'PENCE' points to slightly left of a bead.
- The second 'E' of 'PENCE' points to a space. Some sources consider this to be to the right of a bead.
- The left leg of the 'N' in 'PENCE' points to a bead. Again, some sources consider this to be to slightly right of a bead.
- The right leg of the 'N' points to slightly left of a border bead.
- Small gap between the bottom of the '5' and the beads.
- Small short serifs on the lettering.
- 126 border beads.

Reverse B: Also found on the Proof coins from 1971 to 1979.

- The left leg of the 'N' of 'NEW' points to the right of a border bead.
- The right leg of the 'N' of 'NEW' points to a border bead.
- The 'E' of 'NEW' points to a space.
- The 'P' of 'PENCE' points to the right of a bead.
- The first 'E' of 'PENCE' points to the right of a bead.
- The second 'E' of 'PENCE' points to a border bead.
- The left leg of the 'N' in 'PENCE' points to left of a bead. According to some sources this is to a bead.
- The right leg of the 'N' points to a space. Some sources consider this to be to the right of a bead.
- Wider gap between the bottom of the '5' and the beads.
- Larger longer serifs on the lettering.
- 128 border beads.

Figures 184 – 186, for the 1972 proof five pence illustrate these differentiators, which are not repeated here. Although a definitive differentiator, counting border beads is the least convenient means of establishing the variety of a particular example.

Minor Varieties:

There are no minor design varieties for the 1980 five pence.

1990 Five Pence:

Major Varieties:

There are no major design varieties for the 1990 five pence.

Minor Varieties:

Although there are no specific design varieties for the 1990 five pence, there are two types of edge striking.

The first type has the coin with a so-called wired edge, where the rim of the coin is milled but rounded or bevelled off. The second type has a milled rim, but the edge is cut square.

Figure 189 – 1990 Five Pence Edges

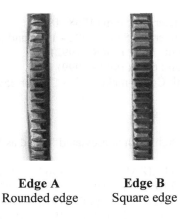

Edge A   **Edge B**
Rounded edge   Square edge

*   *   *   *   *

169

Denomination: Ten Pence

1968 – 1984   1985 – 1992   1992 – 1997   1998 - 1999

1968 – 1981   1982 – 1992   1992 – 1999

Specification: Diameter: 28.5mm (1968 -1992)
Diameter: 24.5mm (1992 - 1999 and to date)
Weight: 11.3g (1968 - 1992)
Weight: 6.5g (1992 - 1999)
Metal: Cupro-nickel (75% Copper/25% Nickel)

Obverse Design:

Elizabeth's bust facing right with abbreviated legend as follows:

1. 'D·G·REG·F·D·(date) ELIZABETH·II' – 1968 – 1984
2. 'ELIZABETH II D·G·REG·F·D·(date)' – 1985 – 1992
3. 'ELIZABETH II D·G REG·F·D·(date)' – 1992 – 1997
4. 'ELIZABETH·II·D·G REG·F·D·(date)' – 1998 – 1999 (then to date)

In 1985 the Queen's bust was changed from the original decimal version by Arnold Machin to a new one by Raphael David Maklouf. This second decimal effigy was used until 1997 after which the third decimal bust (fourth bust of the Queen's reign) designed by Ian Rank-Broadley was introduced.

Reverse Design:

1. A crowned lion passant with '10' below and the inscription 'NEW PENCE' around the top – 1968 – 1981(proof).

2. A crowned lion with '10' below and the inscription 'TEN PENCE' around the top – 1982 – 1999 (large and small flans and to date).

Edge: Milled.

Years Produced: 1968 – 1981 inclusive (except for 1972 and 1978) for the large business strikes and 1992 plus 1995 – 1997 for the smaller coins. Proof sets were produced with a ten pence strike in each year from 1971 to 1999, with large and small coins in the 1992 sets, when the size changeover took place. Uncirculated sets were first produced in 1982 and were an annual issue, each containing uncirculated strikes of the ten pence, regardless of whether these were issued for circulation or not.

Varieties:

Unlike the five pence, which has few varieties, the ten pence coins, from the first in 1968 through to 1977, presents one of the most diverse and peculiar groups of varieties in the entire English coinage series. Several commentators have attempted to catalogue them, with the result that there is a confusing range of descriptors for each variety. Furthermore, there is no obvious logic to the numbering ranges that have been used and no simple correlation between the catalogue numbers based on the different studies made. To make matters even more difficult, there has been a progressive discovery of different varieties over the years which has led to the earlier attempts to catalogue being overtaken by the discoveries, resulting in re-numbering of the types. Finally, there is some dispute and confusion over whether some of the differences found are real or not, and whether they are major or minor varieties. In the early studies there was even a dispute with the Royal Mint over whether certain features actually existed on the coins or not. All this has made describing this series extremely difficult.

There are three main sources for the data on this series. Firstly, there is Davies, which has been used throughout this book as the key catalogue against which other definitions are compared. The second is a study carried out through the early 1970s and culminated in a defining statement in 1978 by K.B.Wiles and E.B.Mackenzie which was reported in Coin Monthly in September 1978. Finally, there is a later study published by R. Stafford, in December 1983, which attempted to define all the types for this series, including proofs and which also cross-referenced to the earlier work of Wiles and Mackenzie.

Because it is extremely difficult to understand the relationship between the obverses and reverses according to each commentator, a table of correlations is provided at Appendix 3. This chart does not provide all the descriptors which are defined in this chapter, but does show which variety is equivalent to which, according to these three sources. In this way, anybody who wishes to study this subject further can readily work out which coin is which according to the source they are using.

Major varieties exist for the business strikes of 1968, 1969, 1970, 1973, 1975, and 1976 and for 1972-1977 inclusively from the proof sets. Minor varieties of the business strikes exist for all the dates in the series from 1968-1977 plus 1979.

For the later smaller sized coins, there are a number of major varieties in 1992 only.

171

1968 Ten Pence

Major Varieties:

The 1968 ten pence has three obverses (obverse 1, obverse 2 and obverse 3) paired to two reverses (reverses A and B) giving the die pairs: 1+A, 1+B, 2+A, 2+B, 3+A and 3+B. Davies catalogues all these types with numbers: 2800, 2801, 2802, 2803, 2804 and 2806. 1+B is unconfirmed by Davies. Davies' descriptions of the three obverse types are similar to other sources, except that many others describe Davies obverse 2 as obverse 3 and Davies obverse 3 as obverse 2. In any comparison of descriptions from different sources, there is the potential for confusion over the numbering of these two types.

Obverses:

Obverse 1:

- The '1' in the date points to a space.
- The 'I' in 'ELIZABETH' points to the right of a bead.
- The apex of the 'A' in 'ELIZABETH' points slightly left of a bead.
- The first upright of the 'H' in 'ELIZABETH' points to a border bead.
- The 'II' has a bead dead centred between the two 'I's.
- The second 'I' in 'II' points to right of a bead.
- The tip of the bust points slightly right of a bead.
- The hair has incuse lines.
- The eyebrow has incuse lines.
- Incuse lines to top of queen's dress.
- Strongly struck high relief head.
- 152 larger border beads closely spaced and away from the rim.

Obverse 2:

- The '1' in the date points slightly to the right of a bead.
- The 'I' in 'ELIZABETH' points slightly to the right of a bead.
- The apex of the 'A' in 'ELIZABETH' points to the right of a bead.
- The first upright of the 'H' in 'ELIZABETH' points to a space.
- The 'II' has a bead left of dead centre between the two 'I's.
- The second 'I' in 'II' points to a space between beads.
- The tip of the bust points to a space.
- The hair has no incuse lines.
- The eyebrow has no incuse lines.
- No incuse lines to top of queen's dress.
- Weakly defined lower relief head.
- 151 border beads, slightly smaller than obverse 1, wider apart and closer to the rim.

172

Obverse 3:

- The '1' in the date points slightly to the right of a bead.
- The 'I' in 'ELIZABETH' points slightly to the right of a bead. Also regarded as to a bead.
- The apex of the 'A' in 'ELIZABETH' points to the right of a bead.
- The first upright of the 'H' in 'ELIZABETH' points to a space.
- The 'II' has a bead left of dead centre between the two 'I's.
- The second 'I' in 'II' points to a space between beads.
- The tip of the bust points to a space.
- The hair has incuse lines.
- The eyebrow has incuse lines – 5 lines.
- Incuse lines to top of queen's dress.
- Well defined but lower relief head.
- 151 border beads, slightly smaller than obverse 1, wider apart and closer to the rim.

There are also suggestions that pointing of the 'R' in 'REG' differs between the three obverses. At best the differences are between slightly left or right of a bead and to a bead, but are very marginal and not the best identifiers for these three types.

Figure 190 – 1968 Ten Pence Obverses (1)

Obverse 1	**Obverses 2&3**
'I' points to a space	'I' points to slightly right of bead

Figure 191 – 1968 Ten Pence Obverses (2)

Obverse 1	**Obverses 2&3**
'I' points to right of bead	'I' points to slightly right of bead
'A' points to slightly left of bead	'A' points to right of bead

173

Figure 192 – 1968 Ten Pence Obverses (3)

Obverse 1
Left leg of 'H' points to bead
'II' has a bead dead centre
Right 'I' points to right of bead

Obverses 2&3
Left leg of 'H' points to a space
'II' has a bead to left of centre
Right 'I' points to a space

Figure 193 – 1968 Ten Pence Obverses (4)

Obverse 1
Tip of bust to right of bead

Obverses 2&3
Tip of bust to space

Figure 194 – 1968 Ten Pence Obverses (5)

Obverses 1&3
5 Incuse eyebrows
Extra lines in hair
Higher relief head
Sharply defined bust

Obverse 2
No incuse eyebrows
Fewer lines in hair
Lower relief head
Weakly defined bust

Figure 195 – 1968 Ten Pence Obverses (6)

Obverse 1	**Obverses 2&3**
Slightly larger beads	Slightly smaller beads
Smaller gap between beads	Larger gaps between beads
Beads away from rim	Beads closer to rim

Figure 196 – 1968 Ten Pence Obverses (7)

Obverses 1&3	**Obverse 2**
Incuse lines in dress	No incuse lines in dress

Reverse A:

- The 'P' in 'PENCE' points to the right of a bead. Sometimes described as being to a space.
- The 'E' of 'PENCE' points to the left of a bead.
- The first upright of the 'N' in 'PENCE' points to slightly right of a bead.
- The lion's nose is flat, wider and has no incuse lines, with no dent to forehead.
- The lion's tail has no incuse lines.
- The left upright of the 'N' in 'NEW' points to a bead.
- The second upright of the 'N' in 'NEW' points to a space.
- The upright of the 'E' in 'NEW' points to left of a bead.
- The lion is well struck in high relief.
- There is a smaller gap between the legend and the design.
- The lettering is slightly thicker.
- The border beads are larger.

Reverse B:

- The 'P' in 'PENCE' points to a bead. Also regarded as slightly to the left of a bead.
- The 'E' of 'PENCE' points to a space.
- The left upright of the 'N' in 'PENCE' points to a bead.
- The lion's nose is sharp, narrower and has incuse lines, giving a 'V' shaped dent to forehead.

175

- The lion's tail has incuse lines.
- The left upright of the 'N' in 'NEW' points to slightly right of a bead.
- The second upright of the 'N' in 'NEW' points to slightly left of a bead.
- The upright of the 'E' in 'NEW' points to a bead.
- The lion is slightly less well struck and in lower relief.
- There is a larger gap between the legend and the design.
- The lettering is slightly thinner.
- The border beads are smaller.

Figure 197 – 1968 Ten Pence Reverses (1)

Reverse A	**Reverse B**
'P' to right of bead	'P' to a bead
'E' points to left of bead	'E' points to a space
Left leg of 'N' to right of bead	Left leg of 'N' to a bead

Figure 198 – 1968 Ten Pence Reverses (2)

Reverse A	**Reverse B**
Flat, wider nose	Sharp, narrow nose
No incuse lines	Incuse lines on nose bridge
Flat forehead	'V' shaped dent in forehead

Figure 199 – 1968 Ten Pence Reverses (3)

Reverse A	**Reverse B**
No extra incuse line	Extra incuse line

Figure 200 – 1968 Ten Pence Reverses (4)

Reverse A	**Reverse B**
Left leg of 'N' to a bead	Left leg to slightly right of bead
Right leg of 'N' to a space	Right leg of 'N' to left of bead
'E' points to left of a bead	'E' points to a bead

Figure 201 – 1968 Ten Pence Reverses (5)

Reverse A	**Reverse B**
Smaller gap, rim to design	Larger gap, rim to design
Thicker lettering	Thinner letters
Larger beads	Smaller beads

Minor Varieties:

There is some dispute among the different sources as to whether obverse 3 is truly a major variety or merely a minor variety of obverse 2. In this book, I have kept with Davies' catalogue which identifies it as a separate major type.

However, there is a minor variety where obverse 3, when paired with reverse A, is

177

found with one of two reverse types:

Variety 3+A Type 1: The normal beaded reverse.
Variety 3+A Type 2: A reverse with some of the upper beads doubled.

Davies catalogues the 3+A as 2804 and the doubled beads type as 2805. In some cases, there are two lines of beads, whilst in others the beads overlap leading to peanut shaped single beads. This also tends to cause the obverse lettering to be thicker than usual with strong square block-like serifs, plus the stops may be oval and elongated vertically.

Figure 202 – 1968 Ten Pence Reverse (6)

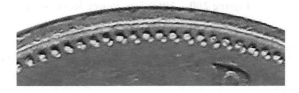

Reverse A – Doubled Beads

1969 Ten Pence:

Major Varieties:

The varieties of the 1969 ten pence proved to be the most difficult to understand and describe in the whole decimal series. Davies does not catalogue any varieties for the 1969 ten pence, regarding them all as having obverse 3 and reverse B i.e. equivalent to the 1968 obverse 3 type. However, in practice, two major types have been found, one having obverse 2 (as for 1968) and the other obverse 3, both coupled with reverse B as for 1968, giving the die pairings 2+B and 3+B.

Obverses:

The identifiers for obverse 2 and 3 are identical to those described earlier for the 1968 ten pence and are not repeated here. They are as illustrated in figures 190 – 196.

Minor Varieties:

Obverses:

For the major variety with obverse 2, reverse B, this type is found as one of two minor obverse types:

Obverse 2 Type 1:

- The pearls on the diadem are large.
- The rim is narrow.

178

Obverse 2 Type 2:

- The pearls on the diadem are smaller.
- The rim is wider.

Figure 203 – 1969 Ten Pence Obverses

Obverse 2 Type 1	**Obverse 2 Type 2**
Larger pearls	Smaller pearls
Thinner rim	Thicker rim

The major type obverse 3 paired with reverse B, as defined by Davies, is catalogued differently by other sources. One defines it as different from the 1968 obverse 3, with one of three different obverses, numbering them obverse 4, obverse 5 and obverse 6, whilst the other is unclear as to whether the reported differences really exist or not, particularly between obverses 5 and 6. This is because the differences are all confined to the measured height of the bust and not to any other features of the design. There are also unresolved issues concerning the reported size of obverses 4 and 5/6, which are alternatively described as 23.75mm versus 24.25 mm and 24.15mm versus 24.4 or 24.5mm. Thus the three types are:

- Obverse 4 – Bust is 24.25mm or 23.75mm
- Obverse 5 – Bust is 24.4mm } or 24.15mm
- Obverse 6 – Bust is 24.5mm } or 24.15mm

For comparison, Davies obverse 3, which is identical in design to the 1968 obverse 3 is reported to have a bust exactly 24mm high, making it slightly different from those for 1969. The measurements refer to the distance from the base of the truncation to the top of the jewels on the front of the diadem, although the precise position on the truncation used to measure was not recorded by those who carried out the measurements. The differences are extremely small and difficult to measure accurately, making it easy to mistake one type for another. Indeed, the differences in size between obverses 5 and 6 are so small as to make it virtually impossible to distinguish them. It is not known whether these three bust sizes are found on the other known major obverse (obverse 2) for this date.

Whether these three are real varieties or simply the result of the margins for error in measuring the bust size or as the result of die wear, there is little doubt that they are minor varieties not major ones.

179

Additionally, for the obverse 4 type, examples are found where the hair and incuse eyebrows are softly struck and some where the strike is clear. There are also two minor varieties of obverse 5/6, based on the cut of the jewels of the diadem:

Obverse 5/6 Type 1:

- The jewels are not clearly cut.
- There are fewer fine lines in the hair etc.
- The diadem pearls are smaller.

Obverse 5/6 Type 2:

- The jewels are very clear.
- The brackets and arcs of the diadem and the curl of hair (extra fine lines in the hair) just below and behind the diadem are both retouched (the scrolls have extra very fine lines in relief).
- Also the diadem pearls are larger and more pronounced.

Further study is needed to determine whether obverse 4 (Davies obverse 3) with the soft strike to the hair and eyebrows has been incorrectly identified as obverse 2 (or vice versa) and whether the type 1 and type 2 minor varieties are found on all bust sizes and types of the 1969 obverse, not just obverse 2 and obverse 5/6.

Reverses:

Although there is only the single reverse B for this year, this is found as one of two minor types:

Reverse B Type 1: With normal rim beads.
Reverse B Type 2: With significant flattening towards the inside.

There are also reports of specimens of the 1969 ten pence, where the die axis is inverted. Normally, the alignment is such that the obverse and reverse are both upright relative to each other, but in some cases the reverse was struck upside down in relation to the obverse. Again, how such specimens correlate with the three obverse types above, and, hence with major obverses 2 and 3, is not known.

Finally, specimens are known where the 'P' of 'PENCE' is missing on the reverse, presumably caused by a blocked die. Again, the correlation of this feature with the possible obverses is not known.

1970 Business Strike Ten Pence:

Major Varieties:

The 1970 currency ten pence has a single obverse (obverse 4) paired to two reverses (reverses B and F) giving the die pairs: 4+B and 4+F. Davies catalogues these with numbers: 2808 and 2809. The 4+F is very rare.

Reverses:

Reverse B:

- The 'P' in 'PENCE' points to the left of a bead. Sometimes regarded as to a bead.
- The 'E' in 'PENCE' points to a space.
- The legend letters are thin, with a wider gap between legend and raised edge.
- Smaller beads.
- The 'E' in 'NEW' points to a bead.
- The left upright of the 'N' in 'NEW' points to slightly right of a bead.
- The second upright of the 'N' in 'NEW' points to left of a bead.
- Centre of the base of the '1' in '10' is slightly to right of a bead.
- Normal sized low relief lion.
- 152 border beads.
- When placed obverse down on a table, the coin lies flat.

Reverse F:

- The 'P' in 'PENCE' points to a bead.
- The 'E' in 'PENCE' points to slightly right of a bead.
- The legend letters are thicker, with a smaller gap from the letters to the edge.
- Larger beads
- The 'E' in 'NEW' points to a space.
- The left upright of the 'N' in 'NEW' points to left of a bead.
- The second upright of the 'N' in 'NEW' points to a space.
- Centre of the base of the '1' in '10' is over a space.
- A small looking lion in high relief.
- 146 border beads.
- When placed obverse down on a table, the coin rocks slightly.

Figure 204 – 1970 Ten Pence Reverses (1)

Reverse B	Reverse F
'P' to left of bead	'P' to a bead
'E' points to a space	'E' points to slightly right of bead
Thin legend letters	Thicker legend letters
Wider gap to edge	Narrower gap to edge
Smaller beads	Larger beads

Figure 205 – 1970 Ten Pence Reverses (2)

Reverse B
'E' points to a bead
1st leg of 'N' points to
slightly right of bead
2nd leg of 'N' points to
left of bead

Reverse F
'E' points to a space
1st leg of 'N' points to
left of bead
2nd leg of 'N' points to
a space

Figure 206 – 1970 Ten Pence Reverses (3)

Reverse B
Centre of '1' over
right of a bead

Reverse F
Centre of '1'over a space

Using the slight differences between the lions or counting border beads are not recommended as the definitive identifiers for these two types.

Minor Varieties:

Davies obverse 4 is considered by one other source to be found as one of two sub-types which are differentiated by the measurement of the bust size (see 1969 ten pences). Obverse 4 is considered to be 24.0mm and the alternative minor type (numbered obverse 7) is measured at 24.25mm, although the precise positions from which the measurement were taken are unspecified. Whether these two minor obverse types are fully paired with the two reverses is unclear.

1971 Business Strike Ten Pence:

Major Varieties:

There are no major design varieties for the 1971 business strike ten pence.

Minor Varieties:

The 1971 ten pence coin is found as one of two minor types:

1. Most coins have the standard rim with the beads away from the rim.
2. Some coins are found with a thick flat rim, which leads to the beads almost touching it.

1972 Proof Strike Ten Pence:

Major Varieties:

The 1972 ten pence was only struck for the proof set and has a single obverse (obverse 7) paired to two reverses (reverses B and E) giving the die pairs: 1+B and 1+E. Davies catalogues these with numbers: 2811 and 2812. The 7+E type is the scarcer of the two.

Reverses:

Reverse B:

- The 'P' in 'PENCE' points to the left of a bead. Also described as to a bead.
- The 'E' in 'PENCE' points to a space.
- The first upright of the 'N' in 'PENCE' points to a bead.
- The second upright of the 'N' in 'PENCE' points to slightly left of a bead.
- The first upright of the 'N' in 'NEW' points to slightly right of a bead.
- The second upright of the 'N' in 'NEW' points to slightly left of a bead.
- The 'E' in 'NEW' points to a bead.
- Centre of the base of the '1' in '10' is slightly to right of a bead.
- Normal sized lower relief lion.
- The lion has a broader face and less dense mane.
- The lion's nose is flat and wider.
- There are incuse lines in the lion's nose.
- The lion has a 'V' shaped dent in the forehead.
- There are longer incuse lines in the lion's tail.
- The legend letters are thicker than on reverse E.
- The rim is thicker.
- The gap from legend to border beads is small.
- The beads are away from the rim.
- The pearls on the lion's crown connect to the crown.

Reverse E:

- The 'P' in 'PENCE' points to the right of a bead.
- The 'E' in 'PENCE' points to a bead.
- The first upright of the 'N' in 'PENCE' points to slightly right of a bead.
- The second upright of the 'N' in 'PENCE' points to a bead.

- The first upright of the 'N' in 'NEW' points to a bead.
- The second upright of the 'N' in 'NEW' points to a space.
- The 'E' in 'NEW' points to slightly left of a bead.
- Centre of the base of the '1' in '10' is slightly to the left of a bead.
- Slightly larger looking higher relief lion.
- The lion has a thinner face and thicker mane.
- The lion's nose is sharp and narrower.
- There are no incuse lines on the bridge of the lion's nose.
- The lion has a flat forehead.
- There are shorter incuse lines in the lion's tail.
- The legend letters are thinner.
- The rim is thinner.
- The gap from legend to border beads is wide.
- The beads are close to the rim.
- The pearls on the lion's crown are clear of the crown.

Figure 207 – 1972 Proof Ten Pence Reverses (1)

Reverse B	**Reverse E**
'P' to left of bead	'P' to right of bead
'E' points to a space	'E' points to a bead
1st leg of 'N' to a bead	1st leg of 'N to slightly right of bead
2nd leg of 'N' to slightly left of bead	2nd leg of 'N' to bead

Figure 208 – 1972 Proof Ten Pence Reverses (2)

Reverse B	**Reverse E**
1st leg of 'N' points to slightly right of bead	1st leg of 'N' points to a bead
2nd leg of 'N' points to slightly left of bead	2nd leg of 'N' points to a space
'E' points to a bead	'E' points slightly left of bead

Figure 209 – 1972 Proof Ten Pence Reverses (3)

Reverse B	**Reverse E**
Centre of '1' is	Centre of '1'is
slightly right of a bead	slightly left of a bead

Figure 210 – 1972 Proof Ten Pence Reverses (4)

Reverse B
Broader face
Less dense mane
Flat, wider nose
Incuse lines on nose
'V' shaped dent in forehead

Reverse E
Thinner face
Denser mane
Sharp, narrow nose
No incuse lines on nose
Flat forehead

Figure 211 – 1972 Proof Ten Pence Reverses (5)

Reverse B
Longer incuse lines

Reverse E
Shorter incuse lines

185

Figure 212 – 1972 Proof Ten Pence Reverses (6)

Reverse B	**Reverse E**
Thick legend letters	Thinner legend letters
Thicker rim	Thinner rim
Small gap letters to beads	Wider gap letters to beads
Beads away from rim	Beads closer to rim

Figure 213 – 1972 Proof Ten Pence Reverses (7)

 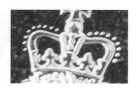

Reverse B	**Reverse E**
Pearls connect to crown	Pearls clear of crown

Minor Varieties:

There are no reported minor varieties for the 1972 proof strike ten pence.

1973 Business Strike Ten Pence:

Major Varieties:

The 1973 ten pence was struck with four obverses (Davies obverse 3, obverse 4, obverse 5 and obverse 6) and three reverses (reverses B, C and D). These are not fully paired giving the die pairs: 3+B, 3+C, 4+B, 5+B, 5+C and 6+D. Davies catalogues these with numbers: 2813, 2814, 2816, 2817, 2818 and 2819. Of these types, the 3+C and 6+D are rare whilst the 5+B and 5+C are very scarce.

Obverses:

Obverse 3:

- The '1' in the date points slightly to the right of a bead.
- The top of the '3' in the date is nearer the rim than the top of the '7'.
- A larger gap between the edge letters and the rim beads.
- The smallest beads for 1973 series.
- Largest gap between beads.

186

- The 'I' of 'ELIZABETH' points to a bead. Also regarded as slightly to the right of a bead.
- The apex of the 'A' in 'ELIZABETH' points to the left of a bead.
- The first upright of the 'H' in 'ELIZABETH' points to a space.
- The second 'I' in 'II' points to a space between beads.
- Beads away from rim.
- The tip of the bust points to a space.
- 151 border beads.
- Thinner lettering in legend.
- Standard rim thickness, thinner than obverse 4.

Obverse 4:

- The '1' in the date points to the left of a bead.
- The tops of the '7' and the '3' in the date are equidistant from the rim.
- A slightly smaller gap between the edge letters and the rim beads.
- There are larger beads than on obverse 3. Largest of 1973 series.
- A smaller gap between beads than on obverse 3. Smallest of the 1973 series.
- The 'I' of 'ELIZABETH' points to slightly left of a bead.
- The 'A' of 'ELIZABETH' points to a bead. Also described as slightly right of a bead.
- The first upright of the 'H' in 'ELIZABETH' points slightly to the right of a bead.
- The second 'I' in 'II' points to a space between beads.
- Beads close to rim.
- The tip of the bust points to a space.
- 151 border beads.
- Thicker lettering in legend.
- Slightly thicker rim than obverse 3.

Obverse 5:

- The '1' in the date points to slightly left of a bead. Also described as to a border bead.
- The tops of the '7' and the '3' in the date are equidistant from the rim.
- A slightly smaller gap between the edge letters and the rim beads.
- Smaller beads than obverse 4, but not as small as obverse 3.
- A wider gap between beads than on obverse 4, but not as wide as for obverse 3.
- The 'I' of 'ELIZABETH' points to slightly right of a bead.
- The 'A' of 'ELIZABETH' points slightly to the left of a bead.
- The first upright of the 'H' in 'ELIZABETH' points to the right of a bead.
- The second 'I' in 'II' points slightly to the left of a bead.
- Beads away from rim.
- The tip of the bust points to a bead.
- 152 border beads.
- Thinner lettering in legend.
- Standard rim thickness, thinner than obverse 4.

Obverse 6:

- The '1' in the date points to a bead.
- The top of the '3' in the date is nearer the rim than the top of the '7'.
- A larger gap between the edge letters and the rim beads.
- Smaller beads than obverse 5, but again not as small as obverse 3.
- Wider gap between beads than on obverse 5, but not as wide as on obverse 3.
- The 'I' of 'ELIZABETH' points to slightly left of a bead.
- The 'A' of 'ELIZABETH' points slightly to the right of a bead.
- The first upright of the 'H' in 'ELIZABETH' points to the right of a bead.
- The second 'I' in 'II' points slightly to the slightly right of a bead.
- Beads away from rim.
- The tip of the bust points to a space.
- 152 border beads.
- Thinner lettering in legend.
- Thinnest rim for this date series.

Figure 214 – 1973 Ten Pence Obverses (1)

Obverse 3	Obverse 4
'I' slightly right of bead	'I' points to left of bead
'3' nearer than '7'	'3' and '7' equidistant
Larger gap legend to beads	Smaller gap legend to beads
Smallest beads for 1973	Largest beads for 1973
Largest gap between beads	Narrowest gap between beads

Obverse 5	Obverse 6
'I' points slightly left of bead	'I' points to a bead
'3' and '7' equidistant	'3' nearer than '7'
Smaller gap legend to beads	Larger gap legend to beads
Intermediate sized beads	Intermediate sized beads
smaller than Obv 4	smaller than Obv 5
Intermediate gap between	Intermediate gap between
beads – wider than Obv 4	beads – wider than Obv 5

188

Figure 215 – 1973 Ten Pence Obverses (2)

Obverse 3
'I' points to a bead
'A' points to left of bead

Obverse 4
'I' points slightly left of bead
'A' points to bead

Obverse 5
'I' points slightly right of bead
'A' points slightly left of a bead

Obverse 6
'I' points slightly left of bead
'A' points slightly right of bead

Figure 216 – 1973 Ten Pence Obverses (3)

Obverse 3
1st leg of 'H' to a space
2nd 'I' points to a space
Beads away from rim

Obverse 4
1st leg of 'H' slightly right of bead
2nd 'I' points to a space
Beads close to rim

Obverse 5
1st leg of 'H' to right of bead
2nd 'I' points slightly left of bead
Beads away from rim

Obverse 6
1st leg of 'H' points right of bead
2nd 'I' points slightly right of bead
Beads away from rim

189

Figure 217 – 1973 Ten Pence Obverses (4)

Obverses 3, 4 & 6
Tip of bust to space

Obverse 5
Tip of bust to bead

As for other denominations, counting border beads is not a recommended means of differentiating the types. The minor variations in rim thickness and legend lettering are also not recommended as a means of distinguishing the four obverses.

Reverses:

Reverse B:

- The 'P' in 'PENCE' points to the left of a bead. Also described as to a bead.
- The 'E' in 'PENCE' points to a space.
- The first upright of the 'N' in 'PENCE' points to a bead.
- The second upright of the 'N' in 'PENCE' points to left of a bead.
- Thinner lettering in legend.
- The first leg of the 'N' in 'NEW' points to slightly right of a bead.
- The second leg of the 'N' in 'NEW' points to slightly left of a bead.
- The leg of the 'E' in 'NEW' points to a bead. Also described as to slightly right of a bead.
- Centre of the base of the '1' in '10' is slightly to right of a bead.
- The legend is furthest from the beaded border of the three types.
- The pearls on the lion's crown are smaller and touching the crown.
- 152 border beads.
- Incuse lines on lion's nose.
- Normal sized low relief lion.

Reverse C:

- The 'P' in 'PENCE' points to the right of a bead. Also described as being to a space by some cataloguers.
- The 'E' in 'PENCE' points to the right of a bead. Also regarded as to a bead.
- The first upright of the 'N' in 'PENCE' points to the right of a bead. Again, some cataloguers regard this as to a bead.
- The second upright of the 'N' in 'PENCE' points to slightly left of a bead.
- Thicker lettering in legend.
- The first leg of the 'N' in 'NEW' points to a bead.
- The second leg of the 'N' in 'NEW' points to slightly right of a bead.
- The leg of the 'E' in 'NEW' points to a space.
- Centre of the base of the '1' in '10' is slightly to the left of a bead.

190

- The legend is nearer the beaded border than on reverse B.
- The pearls on the lion's crown are large, separate but close to the crown.
- 149 border beads.
- No incuse lines on lion's nose.
- A strong, broad faced lion.

Reverse D:

- The 'P' in 'PENCE' points slightly to the left of a bead.
- The 'E' in 'PENCE' points to the right of a bead.
- The first upright of the 'N' in 'PENCE' points to a space.
- The second upright of the 'N' in 'PENCE' points to a bead.
- Thicker lettering in legend.
- The first leg of the 'N' in 'NEW' points to slightly right of a bead.
- The second leg of the 'N' in 'NEW' points to slightly left of a bead.
- The leg of the 'E' in 'NEW' points to a bead.
- Centre of the base of the '1' in '10' is over a bead.
- The legend is nearer the beaded border than on reverse C.
- The pearls on the lion's crown are large, separate but close to the crown.
- 150 border beads.
- Incuse lines on lion's nose.
- Broad faced high relief lion.

Figure 218 – 1973 Ten Pence Reverse (1)

Reverse B	**Reverse C**	**Reverse D**
'P' to left of bead	'P' to right of bead	'P' slightly left of bead
'E' points to a space	'E' points to right of bead	'E' points right of bead
1st leg of 'N' to a bead	1st leg of 'N to right of bead	1st leg of 'N' to space
2nd leg of 'N'	2nd leg of 'N'	2nd leg of 'N'
to left of bead	to slightly left of bead	to a bead
Thinner lettering	Thicker lettering	Thicker lettering

Figure 219 – 1973 Ten Pence Reverses (2)

Reverse B	**Reverse C**	**Reverse D**
1st leg of 'N' points to slightly right of bead	1st leg of 'N' points to a bead	1st leg of the 'N' points slightly right of a bead
2nd leg of 'N' points to slightly left of bead	2nd leg of 'N' points to slightly right of bead	2nd leg of 'N' points to slightly left of bead
'E' points to a bead	'E' points to a space	'E' points to a bead

Figure 220 – 1973 Ten Pence Reverses (3)

Reverse B	**Reverse C**	**Reverse D**
Centre of '1' is slightly right of a bead	Centre of '1'is slightly left of a bead	Centre of '1' is over a bead
Legend away from beads	Legend closer to beads	Legend closest to beads

Figure 221 – 1973 Ten Pence Reverses (4)

Reverse B	**Reverses C&D**
Smaller pearls touching crown	Larger separate pearls close to crown

Counting border beads is not the recommended way to distinguish these types. Also not recommended is the use of the two incuse lines on the lion's nose, since these quickly disappear with wear.

Minor Varieties:

According to Wiles and Mackenzie, but not Stafford, obverse 4 can be considered to be one of two obverses (obverses 9 and 10), the differences relating to the sizes of the bust which are described as 24.25mm and 24.5mm. A second differentiator is the presence of a ledge between the rim beads and the rim. This feature is described in detail at the end of this chapter on the ten pence series.

Also, both obverses 3 and 4 are found as one of two minor varieties:

Type 1: Most coins have the standard thinner rim with the beads away from the rim.
Type 2: Some coins are found with a thick flat rim, which leads to the beads almost touching it.

There are also two types of finish noted for the 1973 coins:

1. Those minted at the Llantrisant mint have a shiny finish.
2. Those minted at the London mint have a matt finish.

The matt finish types are also found with a blurred top of the head and base of the bust.

Finally, there are reports that obverse 3 examples can be found with what are described as 'striations' across the coins. This feature is described at the end of this chapter on the ten pence series.

1973 Proof Strike Ten Pence:

Major Varieties:

The 1973 proof strike ten pence has two obverses (obverse 3 and obverse 9) and two reverses (reverses B and E), which are not fully meshed, giving the die pairings: 3+B, 3+E and 9+E. Davies catalogues these with numbers: 2813, 2815 and 2820. The 9+E type is the rarest of the three types.

Obverses:

Obverse 3:

- The '1' in the date points to the right of a bead.
- The apex of the 'A' in 'ELIZABETH' points to the right of a bead.
- The second 'I' in 'II' points to a space between beads.
- 151 border beads.

Obverse 9:

- The '1' in the date points to a space between border beads.
- The 'A' in 'ELIZABETH' points to a space between beads.
- The second 'I' in 'II' points to a bead.
- 148 border beads.

Figure 222 – 1973 Proof Ten Pence Obverses (1)

Obverse 3
'I' points right of bead

Obverse 9
'I' points to a space

Figure 223 – 1973 Proof Ten Pence Obverses (2)

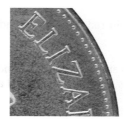 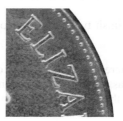

Obverse 3
'A' points to right of bead

Obverse 9
'A' points to a space

Figure 224 – 1973 Proof Ten Pence Obverses (3)

Obverse 3
2ⁿᵈ 'I' points to a space

Obverse 9
2ⁿᵈ 'I' points to a bead

Reverses:

Reverse B:

- The 'P' in 'PENCE' points to the left of a bead. Also described as to a bead.
- The 'E' in 'PENCE' points to a space.
- The first upright of the 'N' in 'PENCE' points to a bead.
- The second upright of the 'N' in 'PENCE' points to slightly left of a bead.
- The first upright of the 'N' in 'NEW' points to slightly right of a bead.

194

- The second upright of the 'N' in 'NEW' points to slightly left of a bead.
- The 'E' in 'NEW' points to a bead.
- Centre of the base of the '1' in '10' is slightly to right of a bead.
- Normal sized low relief lion, with a broader face and less dense mane.
- The lion's nose is flat and wider.
- There are incuse lines in the lion's nose.
- The lion has a 'V' shaped dent in the forehead.
- There are longer incuse lines in the lion's tail.
- The legend letters are thicker than on reverse E.
- The rim is thicker.
- The beads are away from the rim.
- The gap from legend to border beads is small.
- The pearls on the lion's crown connect to the crown.

Reverse E:

- The 'P' in 'PENCE' points to the right of a bead.
- The 'E' in 'PENCE' points to a bead.
- The first upright of the 'N' in 'PENCE' points to slightly right of a bead.
- The second upright of the 'N' in 'PENCE' points to a bead.
- The first upright of the 'N' in 'NEW' points to a bead.
- The second upright of the 'N' in 'NEW' points to a space.
- The 'E' in 'NEW' points slightly to the left of a bead.
- Centre of the base of the '1' in '10' is slightly to the left of a bead.
- Large looking high relief lion, with a thinner face and thicker mane.
- The lion's nose is sharp and narrower.
- There are no incuse lines on the bridge of the lion's nose.
- The lion has a flat forehead.
- There are shorter incuse lines in the lion's tail.
- The legend letters are thinner.
- The rim is thinner.
- The beads are close to the rim.
- The gap from legend to border beads is wide.
- The pearls on the lion's crown are clear of the crown.

These differentiators are illustrated in figures 207 – 213 for the 1972 proof strike ten pences, and are nor repeated here.

Minor Varieties:

There are no reported minor varieties for the 1973 proof strike ten pence.

1974 Business Strike Ten Pence:

Major Varieties:

There are no major design varieties for the 1974 business strike ten pence.

Minor Varieties:

As in the case of the 1973 minor varieties of obverses 3 and 4, the 1974 ten pence coin is found as one of two minor types:

Type 1: Normal, evenly struck obverse.
Type 2: Some coins are found with a blurred top of the head and base of the bust.

This date is also found with the bust in both high relief and lower relief form. All types have the shiny finish. There are also examples struck from a rotated die where the obverse is misaligned with the reverse.

1974 Proof Strike Ten Pence:

Major Varieties:

The 1974 proof strike ten pence has a single obverse (obverse 7) paired with two reverses (reverses B and E) to give the die pairings: 7+B and 7+E. Davies catalogues these with numbers 2822 and 2823. Both types are equally common. The identifiers for the two reverses are identical to those for the 1972 and 1973 proof strike ten pences and are as shown in figures 207 – 213.

Minor Varieties:

There are no reported minor varieties for the 1974 proof strike ten pence.

1975 Business Strike Ten Pence:

Major Varieties:

The 1975 business strike ten pence has a single obverse (obverse 4) paired with two reverses (reverses B and E) to give the die pairings: 4+B and 4+E. Davies catalogues these with numbers 2824 and 2825. The 4+E is the scarcer type.

The identifiers for the two reverses are identical to those for the 1972, 1973 and 1974 (proof strike) ten pences and are as shown in figures 207 – 213 .

Minor Varieties:

As before there are reports that this obverse is found as one of two minor varieties, based on the size of the bust and the shape and existence of ledges between the beads and rim. Davies obverse 4 is equivalent to Stafford's obverse 3 and Wiles and Mackenzie's obverses 9 and 10.

Examples are also known where the normal raised rim is flattened out, almost down to the field of the coin. Specimens occur where the flattening affects both sides of the coin, and also where only one side is impacted. A resulting effect often includes the production of block serifs on the lettering.

1975 Proof Strike Ten Pence:

Major Varieties:

The 1975 proof strike ten pence has, like the business strike, a single obverse (obverse 4) paired with two reverses (reverses B and E) to give the die pairings: 4+B and 4+E. Davies catalogues these with numbers: 2824 and 2825, as for the business coins. The 4+B type is the rarer of the two.

The detailed identifiers are the same as for the business strike and are shown in figures 207 – 213 for the 1972 proof strike.

Minor Varieties:

There are no reported minor varieties for the 1975 proof strike ten pence, even though it has Davies obverse 4.

1976 Business Strike Ten Pence:

Major Varieties:

The 1976 business strike ten pence has a single obverse (obverse 7) paired with two reverses (reverses B and E) to give the die pairings: 7+B and 7+E. Davies catalogues these with numbers: 2826 and 2827. The 7+E variety is the scarcer.

The identifiers for the two reverses are identical to those for the 1972 (proof), 1973 (proof), 1974 (proof) and 1975 (business and proof) ten pences, and are as shown in figures 207 – 213.

Minor Varieties:

As for the 1975 business strike, examples are known where the normal raised rim is flattened out, almost down to the field of the coin. Specimens occur where the flattening affects both sides of the coin, and also where only one side is impacted.

1976 Proof Strike Ten Pence:

Major Varieties:

The 1976 proof strike ten pence has, like the business strike, a single obverse (obverse 7) paired with two reverses (reverses B and E) to give the die pairings: 7+B and 7+E. Davies catalogues these with numbers: 2826 and 2827, as for the business coins. The 7+B type is the scarcer.

The identifiers for the two reverses are again identical to those for the 1972 (proof), 1973 (proof), 1974 (proof) and 1975 (business and proof) ten pences, and are as shown in figures 207 – 213.

Minor Varieties:

There are no reported minor varieties for the 1976 proof strike ten pence.

1977 Business Strike Ten Pence:

Major Varieties:

There are no reported major varieties for the 1977 business strike ten pence, which has obverse 3 paired with reverse B, giving the single die pair 3+B, and with catalogue number 2828.

Minor Varieties:

The 1977 ten pence is found as one of two minor varieties:

Reverse B Type 1: The incuse line on the lion's nose extends downwards to about midway between the eyes. This is the common type for this year.
Reverse B Type 2: The incuse line on the lion's nose extends right down the nose, dividing it in two.

1977 Proof Strike Ten Pence:

Major Varieties:

The 1977 proof strike ten pence has two obverses (obverse 8 and obverse 10) paired with a single reverse (reverse E) to give the die pairings: 8+E and 10+E. Davies catalogues these with numbers 2829 and 2830. The 8+E type is the scarcer.

Obverses:

Obverse 8:

- The '1' in 'the date to points to a space.
- The 'I' of 'ELIZABETH' points to right of a bead.
- The 'A' in 'ELIZABETH' points to a space between beads.
- The first upright of the 'H' in 'ELIZABETH' points to right of a bead.
- The second upright of the 'H' in 'ELIZABETH' points to a space.
- The last 'I' in 'II' points to slightly right of a border bead.
- The tip of the truncation to a bead.
- A higher relief head.
- Less deeply cut and fewer hair lines.
- 148 larger border beads.
- A thicker rim.
- A slightly smaller gap between beads.
- The beads are away from the rim.

Obverse 10:

- The '1' in the date to slightly left of a border bead.
- The 'I' of 'ELIZABETH' points to a space.
- The 'A' in 'ELIZABETH' points to the left of a bead.
- The first upright of the 'H' in 'ELIZABETH' points to a space.
- The second upright of the 'H' in 'ELIZABETH' points to left of a bead.
- The last 'I' in 'II' points to the right of a border bead.
- The tip of the truncation to a space.
- Lower relief head.
- Deep cut and extra incuse hair lines.
- 147 slightly smaller border beads.
- A thinner rim.
- A larger gap between beads.
- The beads are closer to the rim.

Figure 225 – 1977 Proof Ten Pence Obverses (1)

Obverse 8	**Obverse 10**
'I' points to a space	'I' points to slightly left of bead

Figure 226 – 1977 Proof Ten Pence Obverses (2)

Obverse 8	**Obverse 10**
'I' points to right of bead	'I' points to a space
'A' points to a space	'A' points to left of bead

Figure 227 – 1977 Proof Ten Pence Obverses (3)

Obverse 8
Left 'H' points to right of bead
Right 'H' points to a space
2nd 'I' points slightly right of bead

Obverse 10
Left 'H' points to a space
Right 'H' points to left of bead
2nd 'I' points right of a bead

Figure 228 – 1977 Proof Ten Pence Obverses (4)

Obverse 8
Tip of bust to a bead

Obverse 10
Tip of bust to space

Figure 229 – 1977 Proof Ten Pence Obverses (5)

Obverse 8
Higher relief head
Less deeply cut lines
Fewer lines in hair

Obverse 10
Lower relief head
Deeper cut lines
More lines in hair

Figure 230 – 1977 Proof Ten Pence Obverses (6)

Obverse 8	Obverse 10
Slightly larger beads	Slightly smaller beads
Thicker rim	Thinner rim
Smaller gap between beads	Larger gap between beads
Beads away from rim	Beads closer to rim

Minor Varieties:

There are no reported minor varieties for the 1977 proof strike ten pence.

1979 Proof Strike Ten Pence:

Major Varieties:

There are no reported major varieties for the 1979 proof strike ten pence, which has obverse 10 paired with reverse E, giving the single die pair 10+E, and with catalogue number 2833.

Minor Varieties:

Two minor types of 1979 proof ten pence have been reported:

Reverse E Type 1: The 'normal' or common type has reverse E, as found on the other proof sets of the early 1970s. This type is characterised by:

- A wider rim.
- Larger rim beads.
- A larger crown to the lion.
- A higher relief design and sharply struck inscription.

Reverse E Type 2: The much rarer type is similar to the usual Reverse E, but has:

- A narrower rim.
- Smaller rim beads.
- A smaller crown to the lion.
- A slightly lower relief design and less well struck inscription.

The obverse of the rarer type is unusual in that it is found with a distinctive V-shaped raised punch mark just in front of the queen's ear on her cheek. This feature has been

201

queried with the Royal Mint, eliciting the explanation that this was the result of a 'Vicker's hardness check'. It was originally thought that this check was carried out on the coin or coin blank but the position suggests that it would not be a blank that was punched, as the alignment on the coin is too well camouflaged. Possibly an individual coin was punched, but this doesn't explain exactly why such a test would be necessary on a struck coin. More likely, the working die was punched as a test of its hardness i.e its fitness for purpose, and the subsequent mark polished out. This idea is supported by the existence of fine incuse hair lines where the 'V' should be on the more common type coins and the general contours of the face in this area. If this is correct then it also suggests that at least one working die did not have its punched test disfiguration polished out by the mint, leading to the coins of type 2.

1992 Business Strike Ten Pence:

Davies' book, 'British Silver Coins' was first published in 1982 and for this reason does not catalogue coins beyond 1980. However, the system used by Davies describes the obverse varieties of a single design type using digit numbering starting at obverse 1 and lettering for the reverses starting at reverse A. When a change in fundamental design change occurs, Davies re-starts the numbering at obverse 1/reverse A. This means that, when the size of the ten pence coins changed in 1992, it is appropriate and consistent with Davies' approach, to commence the numbering of the designs for that year at obverse 1 and reverse A, and base any varieties on this start point.

Major Varieties:

For 1992, there are two obverses (obverse 1 and obverse 2) and two reverses (reverse A and reverse B). These are fully coupled to give the die pairs 1+A, 1+B, 2+A and 2+B. Additionally, there are two types of edge found on these coins. The earlier ones had a 'wired' or rounded edge, whilst the later coins had a straight and wider edge. The 'wired' edge type is only found with the die pairing 1+A. Thus there are five types of 1992 circulating ten pence. The 2+B type is the one found in the proof and uncirculated sets.

Obverses:

Obverse 1:

- The 'L' in 'ELIZABETH' points to a space between beads.
- The 'I' in 'ELIZABETH' points to a space between beads.

Obverse 2:

- The 'L' in 'ELIZABETH' points to a border bead.
- The 'I' in 'ELIZABETH' points to left of a border bead (described by some as to a bead).

Figure 231 – 1992 Ten Pence Obverses

Obverse 1
'L' points to a space
'I' points to a space

Obverse 2
'L' points to a bead
'I' points to left of bead

Reverses:

Reverse A:

- The '1' in '10' points directly to, but slightly right of a border bead.

Reverse B:

- The '1' in '10' points to a space between border beads.

Figure 232 – 1992 Ten Pence Reverses

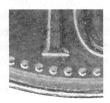 

Reverse A
'1' points slightly right of bead

Reverse B
'1' points to a space

Edges:

Figure 233 – 1992 Ten Pence Edges

Rounded edge

Flat edge

203

Minor Varieties:

There are no reported minor varieties of the 1992 currency ten pence.

Ledges:

For the obverse of coins dated between 1973 and 1976, early studies showed differences in the area between the border beads and the edge of the coin. In the case of currency coins minted between 1968 and 1971 the rim rises directly from the flan, with no ledge. In the case of the coins dated from 1973 to 1981, coins were found to have a distinct ledge between the beads and the rim. Additionally, the ledges were found to be either plain or scalloped behind the beads, with metal flow around the back of the beads. Both types do not automatically occur in each year and for each variety as described in this chapter.

When this issue was first raised with the Royal Mint, they initially decided that the existence of the ledges was illusory. This was because although they had made no change to the minting process, they had changed the finish of the dies, which were Chrome plated from 1973. This was thought to have softened the angle between the rim and the beading, leading to reflections from the highlighted bevel which appeared as a ledge.

When further enquiries were made, the Royal Mint considered the matter further and reported that the ledges were probably the result of changes they had made to the die-making procedures. Apparently, the earlier practice was to employ two blows to sink a die from a working punch, but this process was changed to enable a single process to transfer the design from the punch to the die. The new procedure affected the metal flow when the die was made and produced a weakness inside the edge of a coin. The Mint suggested that the shape of the ledge was related to the width of the flat area between the beads and the edge. Basically, where the gap is narrow, the ledge will be scalloped and the beads not fully formed, whereas with a wider gap, the scalloped effect disappears and the beads are fully rounded. The Royal Mint also commented that the proof dies were still made under the old two-stage process and would not be expected to show this effect, which is exactly what was found up until 1977, when both scalloped and flat ledge types were found on the obverse.

If this is the correct explanation, then it is a slightly unusual case where a variety has arisen by accident through a process change, rather than some alteration to the design.

Figure 234 – 1970s Ledges

No ledge   **Scalloped ledge**   **Plain ledge**

The known distribution of ledges is as follows:

Business Strikes:

Obverses:

1968:   Obv 1:   No ledge
            Obv 2:   No ledge
            Obv 3:   No ledge

1969:   Obv 3:   No ledge

1970:   Obv 4:   No ledge

1971:   Obv 4:   No ledge

1973:   Obv 3:   Plain ledge
                     Scalloped ledge
            Obv 4:   Plain ledge   } Both types are found on the 24.25mm bust
                     Scalloped ledge   } minor variety
                     No ledge   } Not found on the 24.5mm bust type.
            Obv 5:   Plain ledge
                     Scalloped ledge
            Obv 6:   Plain ledge
                     Scalloped ledge

1974:   Obv 3:   Plain ledge
                     Scalloped ledge

1975:   Obv 4:   Plain ledge   } Both types are found on the 24.25mm bust
                     Scalloped ledge   }   minor variety
                     No ledge   } On the 24.5mm bust type only.

1976:   Obv 7:   Plain ledge   } When paired with reverse B.
                     Plain ledge   } When paired with reverse E.
                     Scalloped ledge   } When paired with reverse E.

1977:   Obv 3:   Scalloped ledge

1979:   Obv 10: Scalloped ledge

1980:   Obv 10: Scalloped ledge

1981:   Obv 10: Plain ledge

Reverses:

1968: Rev A: No ledge
       Rev B: No ledge

1969: Rev B: No ledge

1970: Rev B: No ledge
       Rev F: No ledge

1971: Rev B: No ledge

1973: Rev B: No ledge
       Rev C: Plain ledge
       Rev D: Plain ledge

1974: Rev B: No ledge

1975: Rev B: No ledge   } Both types are found on the 24.25mm and
               Plain ledge   } 24.5mm obverse bust minor varieties.
               Scalloped ledge
       Rev E: Plain ledge

1976: Rev B: No ledge
               Plain ledge
       Rev E: Plain ledge

1977: Rev B: Plain ledge

1979: Rev B: No ledge

1980: Rev B: No ledge

1981: Rev B: No ledge

Proof Strikes:

For the coins in the early proof series, there are no ledges of either type found on either the obverse or reverse. The one exception is in 1977, where obverse 8 only is found with both plain and scalloped ledges.

From 1978 to 1980, plain ledges are found on the reverses and obverses of suggesting that the Royal Mint changed over to the single stage die sinking process for proofs as well as business strikes. However, there do not seem to be any with scalloped edges, suggesting that they managed to eliminate this particular feature.

Clogged Dies:

These are a fairly common fault caused by a build up of grease in the dies resulting in parts of the struck design to be faint or missing. Examples are found on the 1968 2+A, 3+B, 1969, 1974, 1975 4+B, 1976 7+B and 7+E types.

Doubling:

Apart from the well known doubling of beads on the 1968 2+A type, both major and minor doublings occur throughout the series, caused by hubbing errors in the production of new dies. Dates/die pairs where this is known include business strikes of 1968 2+A, 1969, 1970, 1973 3+B and 4+B, 1974, 1975 4+B and 4+E, 1976 7+B and 7+E.

Die Cracks:

Die cracks are rare on the decimal series of any denomination. However, there are specimens known of the 1976 7+B type.

Readers who are interested in these mistrikes should consult reference no.32 at appendix 2 for detailed information about the details of the errors for each date and type.

Striations:

The ten pence coins of certain years show a curious feature of having striations across the flan. In particular this effect is present on 1971, 1975 and some 1973 coins, in particular those with obverse 4.

Sharp Serifs:

Another feature found on coins through the early dates for the ten pence series is the presence of blunt and sharp serifs on the legend letters. In some examples the serifs at the end of the letters are quite pointed and well defined even on worn specimens. In other cases the ends of the serifs are blunter and more rounded. It has been suggested that this is not a design feature of the coins, but is a further consequence of the changes made to the dies, which led to the different ledge types mentioned above. This is borne out by the illustration in figure 235, where there are sharper serifs on the plain ledge type and blunt serifs on the scalloped ledge, the theory being that the metal flow leading to the scallops did not leave sufficient metal for the serifs to be fully struck up. Further study is needed to establish exactly which dates and ledge types exhibit this feature.

Figure 235 – 1970s Serifs

Sharp serifs   **Blunt serifs**

*   *   *   *   *

Denomination: Twenty Pence

1982 – 1984	1985 – 1997	1998 – 1999

1982 – 1999

Specification: Diameter: 21.4mm (across corner to curved edge)
Weight: 5.0g
Metal: Cupro-nickel (84% Copper, 16% Nickel)

Obverse Design:

A seven sided, curved edge coin, with Elizabeth's bust facing right with abbreviated legend as follows:

1. 'ELIZABETH II D·G·REG·F·D·' – 1982 – 1997 (and to 2008)
2. 'ELIZABETH II D·G·REG·F·D' – 1997 – 1999 (and to 2008)

Reverse Design:

A crowned double rose, which divides the date, with the words 'TWENTY PENCE' around the top of the coin, and the number '20' at the bottom.

Edge: Plain seven sided curved.

Years Produced:

For circulation, the twenty pence was first introduced in 1982 and was issued in every year since (except 1986) up to and including 2008. Over this period, the obverse effigy has changed from the original Arnold Machin young portrait, to the Raphael Maklouf portrait in 1985, to the older effigy by Ian Rank-Broadley in 1998, whilst the reverse design has remained unchanged, apart from the date. During this time, the Royal Mint started to produce 'Brilliant Uncirculated' sets of coins in each year and so there is a 1986 twenty pence coin found in this set. Similarly, they also produced proof coin sets in each year and again the twenty pence piece was included in each year.

Varieties:

Despite the production of twenty pence coins as both business strikes and for the uncirculated and proof sets over a 18 year period of the 20th century, a major variety only exists for 1992 and there are no reported minor types at all.

1992 Business Strike Twenty Pence

Major Varieties:

The 1992 business strike has two obverses (obverse 2 and obverse 3) paired with a single reverse (reverse A) to give the die pairings: 2+A and 3+A. Obverse 2 is found on coins from 1985 until 1992, when the size of the bust was changed. Obverse 3 with the slightly larger bust is then found on coins from 1992 to 1997, when obverse 4 was produced. The 2+A type is the scarcer.

Obverses:

Obverse 2:

- The top of the diadem is away from the inner ridge.
- A smaller bust – roughly 13.5mm from diadem to tip of truncation.
- Low relief poorly struck portrait.
- The tip of the truncation is away from the edge ridge.

Obverse 3:

- The top of the diadem is nearer the inner ridge.
- A larger bust – approximately 14mm from diadem to tip of the truncation.
- Higher relief well struck portrait.
- The tip of the truncation is closer to the edge ridge.

Figure 236 – 1992 Twenty Pence Obverses (1)

 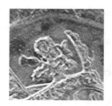

Obverse 2	Obverse 3
Diadem away from inner ridge	Diadem close to inner ridge

Figure 237 – 1992 Twenty Pence Obverses (2)

Obverse 2	**Obverse 3**
Smaller bust	Larger bust
Low relief head	High relief head
Poor strike	Well struck

Figure 238 – 1992 Twenty Pence Obverses (3)

 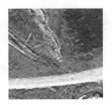

Obverse 2	**Obverse 3**
Truncation away from ridge	Truncation close to ridge

Minor Varieties:

There are no minor varieties for this date.

*   *   *   *   *

Denomination: Twenty Five Pence

1972 Elizabeth & Philip Crown

1977 Jubilee Crown

1980 Queen Mother's 80th Birthday

1981 Wedding of Charles and Diana

Specification: Diameter: 38.6mm
                         Weight: 28.3g
                         Metal: Cupro-nickel (75% Copper, 25% Nickel)

Obverse Design:

1. Elizabeth's bust facing right with abbreviated legend as follows:
'D·G·REG·F·D·ELIZABETH II' – 1972, 1980 and 1981

2. Elizabeth, on horseback, riding to the left, with the legend: 'ELIZABETH·II
DG·REG FD 1977' – 1977

Reverse Design:

1. EP on a floral motif with a crown above and the inscription 'ELIZABETH AND
PHILIP' around the top and '20 NOVEMBER 1947-1972' – 1972 only.

2. A stylised ampulla and anointing spoon as used at the coronation in 1953, with a
crown above and surrounded by a floral border – 1977 only.

3. The bust of the Queen Mother facing left at the centre, within a decoration and
with the words 'QUEEN ELIZABETH THE QUEEN MOTHER' around the top and
'AUGUST 4th 1980' around the bottom – 1980 only.

4. The conjoined busts of Charles and Diana facing left, plus the inscription 'HRH
THE PRINCE OF WALES AND LADY DIANA SPENCER' and 1981 below –
1981 only.

Edge: Milled.

Years Produced:

As commemoratives these were all one year type coins struck for specific events.
The 1977, 1980 and 1981 coins were also issued to specimen standards in a card
holder. Additionally, the 1972 and 1977 coins were included in the proof sets of
those years. Each type is also available as a sterling silver proof, usually boxed.

Varieties:

Despite the huge numbers of these coins that were produced, only the 1977 crown is
found with minor varieties.

1977 Commemorative Strike Twenty Five Pence

Major Varieties:

There are no major varieties for this date.

Minor Varieties:

The obverse of the 1977 crown is found as one of two types:

Obverse Type 1: This has larger beads to the inner circle and as a consequence the beads are closer to the legend.

Obverse 1 Type 2: This type has smaller beads and the gap between the beads and legend is larger.

Figure 239 – 1977 Crown Obverses

Type 1	**Type 2**
Larger beads	Smaller beads
Small gap to legend	Wider gap to legend

*   *   *   *   *

Denomination: Fifty Pence

1969 – 1984   1985 – 1997   1997   1998 – 1999

1969 – 1981   1973   1982 – 1997

1992/93   1994   1997

1998   1998

Specification: Diameter: 30mm (across corner to curved edge)
Diameter: 27.3mm (across corner to curved edge)
Weight: 13.5g
Weight: 8.0g
Metal: Cupro-nickel (75% Copper, 25% Nickel)

Obverse Designs:

A seven sided, curved edge coin, with Elizabeth's bust facing right with abbreviated
legend as follows:

1. 'D·G·REG·F·D·date ELIZABETH·II' – 1969 – 1984
2. 'ELIZABETH II D·G·REG·F·D·date' – 1985 – 1997

215

3. 'ELIZABETH II D·G·REG·F·D·date' – 1997 only (smaller size)
4. 'ELIZABETH·II·D·G REG·F·D·date' – 1998 – 1999 (and to 2008)

The original bust from 1969 until 1984 was the first decimal version designed by Arnold Machin. Along with other denominations, this was changed in 1985 to a new one by Raphael David Maklouf. This second decimal effigy was used until 1997 after which the third decimal bust (fourth bust of the Queen's reign) designed by Ian Rank-Broadley was introduced. From 1997, the new smaller sized fifty pence piece was used.

Reverse Designs:

1. Seated Britannia with '50' below and the words 'NEW PENCE' around the top – 1969 – 1981 (except 1973).
2. Nine clasped hands in a circle, with the words '1973 50 PENCE' in the centre – 1973 only.
3. Seated Britannia with '50' below and the words 'FIFTY PENCE' around the top – 1982 - 1997 (large flan).
4. Stylised conference table with seats around and 12 stars in the centre, plus the inscription '1992   UK   1993' around the top and '50 PENCE' at the bottom – 1992 and 1993.
5. A stylised invasion force of planes and ships, for the 50th anniversary of D-Day, with '50 PENCE' on the lower right side – 1994.
6. Seated Britannia with '50' below and the words 'FIFTY PENCE' around the top – 1997 – 1999 (and up to 2008) (small flan).
7. Twelve stars arranged as a fireworks pattern, with the words '1973   EU   1998' just above '50 PENCE' at the bottom of the coin – 1998.
8. A pair of hands holding the sun's rays inside a circle with the inscription 'FIFTIETH ANNIVERSARY' inside at the top and '50' at the bottom. Around the outside of the circle the initials 'NHS' five times and 'PENCE' at the bottom – 1998.

Edge: Plain seven side curved, known as a Reuleaux polygon type.

Years Produced:

Fifty pence pieces with the early decimal head and the 'NEW PENCE' reverse were produced for all years as business strikes from 1969 to 1981, except the period from 1971 to 1975. From 1982 to 1984, business strikes were produced, except for 1984, and were identical to the earlier coins except that the reverse inscription was changed to 'FIFTY PENCE'. Additionally, the uncirculated sets from 1982 to 1984 also contained the same type coins.

Similarly, coins from all the proof sets, except 1973, from 1971 through to 1981 were struck with the first decimal bust and the 'NEW PENCE' Britannia reverse. As for the business and uncirculated set types, the proof sets from 1982 to 1984 have the first decimal bust and 'FIFTY PENCE' Britannia reverse.

From 1985 through to 1997 the second decimal bust was used for all currency coins. The Britannia reverse is present on the business strike of 1985 and in the uncirculated sets from 1985 through to 1997, except for 1994. This type is also found on coins from the proof sets over this same period, again with the exception of 1994.

For 1997, the second decimal bust was used with the Britannia reverse and the new smaller flan to produce a 'one year type' business strike coin. This type is also found in the uncirculated and proof sets of that year, together with the large flan types.

From 1998 and to date, the third and older decimal bust was used. Business strike Britannia reverses were produced for 1998 and 1999, and these are also present in both the uncirculated and proof sets.

The commemorative reverses are 'one year types' found on the coins of 1973, 1992-93, 1994, and 1998 (two coins). The 1973 'hands' reverse is found as a circulating coin as well as a proof strike. However, the 1992-3 and 1994 coins were not usually circulated and are found in the proof sets of 1992 and 1994, as well as in the uncirculated sets of these years. Unusually, the 1992-3 coin is also found in the 1993 uncirculated set as well as for 1992. For 1998, the EU fifty pence coin is a circulating coin and is also found in the proof and uncirculated sets. However, the NHS commemorative of the same year is found as a circulating coin only and is not present in either of the sets. It is available as a specimen in a presentation folder and as a singleton proof in various metals. The other commemoratives are also generally available in presentation folders and in silver, gold etc.

Varieties:

Major varieties are known for the 1969, 1976, 1979 and 1981 business strikes and for the 1972, 1973, 1974, 1975 and 1976 proof strikes. Minor varieties occur in 1969, 1977 and 1979 for the business strikes.

1969 Fifty Pence:

Major Varieties:

The 1969 business fifty pence has two obverses, designated by Davies as obverse 1 and obverse 2, each paired with a single reverse (reverse A), giving the die pairs 1+A and 2+A. These are catalogued by Davies with numbers 2700 and 2701 respectively.

Obverses:

Obverse 1:

- Smaller design than obverse 2 – approximately 24mm from base to diadem.
- There is more space between the left hand lettering and the raised rim.
- There is a narrower gap between the legend and the right rim.
- The bust and baseline are slightly better defined.

Obverse 2:

- Larger design than obverse 1 – approximately 24.5mm from base to diadem.
- There is a smaller gap between the left hand lettering and the raised rim.
- There is a wider space between the right hand lettering and the raised rim. This means that there is even spacing between the legend and the raised rim all round the coin.
- The bust and its base line are less well defined.

The type with the smaller head (obverse 1) is scarcer than the other. Of these identifiers the spacing of the legend from the rim is by far the most definitive, although the size of the bust is immediately obvious when specimens of both types are in the hand.

Figure 240 – 1969 Fifty Pence Obverses (1)

Obverse 1	Obverse 2
More space left legend to edge	Smaller space left legend to edge

Figure 241 – 1969 Fifty Pence Obverses (2)

Obverse 1	Obverse 2
Narrow gap right legend to edge	Wider space right legend to edge

Minor Varieties:

The major variety with obverse 1 is found as one of two minor types:

Obverse 1 Type 1: The normal type with weakly struck incuse lines in the hair.
Obverse 1 Type 2: A scarcer type with more sharply cut and extra incuse lines.

Figure 242 – 1969 Fifty Pence Obverses (3)

Obverse 1 –Type 1
Weakly struck
incuse lines

Obverse 1 – Type 2 & Obverse 2
Sharply cut
incuse lines

The major variety with obverse 2 is also found as one of two minor reverse types:

Obverse 2 Type A: Britannia's head and helmet are normal sized.
Obverse 2 Type B: Britannia's head and helmet are smaller.

There are also error coins of 1969 where the obverse was struck on both sides, plus there are undated errors where double tailed coins were produced.

1972 Proof Strike Fifty Pence:

Major Varieties:

There are no major varieties identified for this year and strike by Davies, which is catalogued as having obverse 4, reverse B with number 2704. However, two different reverses have been described, the 'thinner' design and the 'thicker' type. The 'thinner' type is the scarcer of the two.

Thinner Reverse:

- Has a standard width for Britannia's waist.
- Has a thinner upper arm than the 'thicker' design.

Thicker Reverse:

- Has a thicker width for Britannia's waist.
- Has a thicker upper arm than the 'thinner' design.

Figure 243 – 1972 Proof Fifty Pence Reverses

Normal Reverse	**Thicker Reverse**
Standard waist	Wider waist
Thinner arm	Thicker arm

Minor Varieties:

There are no minor varieties for the 1972 proof fifty pence.

1973 Proof Strike Fifty Pence:

Major Varieties:

Davies catalogues a single type for the 1973 proof strike fifty pence commemorating 'Accession to the European Economic Community' with the clasped hands reverse and number 2750. However, a small number of coins were struck in silver on thicker flans, but not piedfort weight, for presentation to EEC Finance Ministers and other officials on the occasion of Britain joining the EEC.

Minor Varieties:

There are no minor varieties for the 1973 proof fifty pence.

1974 Proof Strike Fifty Pence:

Major Varieties:

There are no major varieties identified by Davies for the proof fifty pence, which is catalogued as having obverse 4, reverse B with number 2705. However, as for the 1972 proof coin, two different reverses have been described, the 'thinner' design and the 'thicker' type. The identifiers are as shown in figure 243 for 1972. The 'thinner' type is the scarcer of the two.

Minor Varieties:

There are no minor varieties for the 1974 proof fifty pence.

1975 Proof Strike Fifty Pence:

Major Varieties:

There are no major varieties identified by Davies for the proof fifty pence, which is catalogued as having obverse 4, reverse B with number 2706. However, as for the 1972 and 1974 proof coins, two different reverses have been described, the 'thinner' design and the 'thicker' type. The identifiers are as shown in figure 243 for 1972. The 'thinner' type is the scarcer of the two.

Minor Varieties:

There are no minor varieties for the 1975 proof fifty pence.

1976 Business Strike Fifty Pence:

Major Varieties:

Davies catalogues a single obverse (obverse 3) for the 1976 business strike fifty pence, and two reverses (reverse A and reverse B), giving the die pairs 3+A and 3+B. These are numbered 2707 and 2708 respectively. These reverses are again the 'thinner' design and the 'thicker' type, but with additional identifiers:

Reverse A:

- The legend letters are larger.
- The legend is closer to the border.
- Has a standard width for Britannia's waist.
- Has a thinner upper arm than the 'thicker' design.
- The background area in the crook of the arm is large.

Reverse B:

- The legend letters are small.
- The legend letters are away from the border.
- Has a thicker width for Britannia's waist.
- Has a thicker upper arm than the 'thinner' design.
- The background area in the crook of the arm is small.

The 3+B type is very much scarcer.

Figure 244 – 1976 Business Strike Fifty Pence Obverses

Reverse A	**Reverse B**
Larger legend letters	Smaller legend letters
Letters close to border	Letters away from border

Figure 245 – 1976 Business Strike Fifty Pence Obverses

Reverse A	**Reverse B**
Standard waist	Wider waist
Thinner arm	Thicker arm
Crook of arm is large	Crook of arm is small

Minor Varieties:

There are no minor varieties for the 1976 business strike fifty pence.

1976 Proof Strike Fifty Pence:

Major Varieties:

There are no major varieties identified by Davies for the proof fifty pence, which is catalogued as having obverse 3, reverse B with number 2708. However, as for the 1972, 1974 and 1975 proof coins, two different reverses have been described, the 'thinner' design and the 'thicker' type. The identifiers are as shown in figure 243 for 1972. The 'thinner' type is considerably the scarcer of the two.

Minor Varieties:

There are no minor varieties for the 1976 proof fifty pence.

1977 Business Strike Fifty Pence:

Major Varieties:

There are no major varieties for the 1977 business strike fifty pence, which is catalogued by Davies with obverse 4, reverse A and number 2709.

Minor Varieties:

There are two minor varieties of the 1977 business strike coin, based on the alignment of the date numerals:

Obverse 4 Type 1: The common type is where the '1' and the '9' in the date are parallel to each other.
Obverse 4 Type 2 : The rarer type has the '1' and the '9' misaligned.

1979 Business Strike Fifty Pence:

Major Varieties:

Davies identifies the 1979 business strike as having a single obverse (obverse 5) coupled with one of two reverses (reverse A and reverse B), giving the die pairs 5+A and 5+B. These are catalogued with numbers 2713 and 2714 respectively. These two reverses are described earlier for 1976 and are illustrated in figures 244 and 245.

Minor Varieties:

There are two minor varieties of the 1979 business strike coin with reverse A, based on the spacing of the date numerals:

Reverse A Type 1: The common type has a widely spaced date with the 'thinner' reverse design.
Reverse A Type 2: The rarer type has a closely spaced date, again with the 'thinner' reverse.

The 'thicker' design type (reverse B) is only found with the widely spaced date.

1981 Business Strike Fifty Pence:

Major Varieties:

As for the 1979 fifty pence, the 1981 business strike has a single obverse (obverse 5) coupled to two reverses (reverse A and reverse B), giving the die pairs 5+A and 5+B. These are beyond Davies' catalogue system and are thus not numbered. These two reverses are the 'thinner' and 'thicker' reverse types, as described earlier for 1976 and are illustrated in figures 244 and 245.

Minor Varieties:

There are no minor varieties of the 1981 business strike coin.

*   *   *   *   *

Denomination: One Pound

1983-4   1985-1997   1998-1999

1983, 1993, 1998   1984, 1989   1985, 1990   1986, 1991

1987, 1992   1988   1994, 1999

1995   1996   1997

Specification: Diameter: 22.5mm
Weight: 9.5g
Metal: Nickel-brass

Obverse Designs:

1. 'D·G·REG·F·D·Date ELIZABETH·II' – 1983 – 1984
2. 'ELIZABETH II D·G·REG·F·D·date' – 1985 – 1997
3. 'ELIZABETH·II·D·G REG·F·D·date' – 1998 – 1999 (and to date)

The original bust used in 1983 and 1984 was the first decimal type designed by Arnold Machin. Along with other denominations, this was changed in 1985 to a new one by Raphael David Maklouf. This second decimal effigy was used until 1997 after which the third decimal bust (fourth bust of the Queen's reign) designed by Ian Rank-Broadley was introduced.

Reverse Designs:

1. The royal arms with the legend 'ONE POUND' underneath – 1983, 1993 and 1998
2. A thistle plant inside a coronet (for Scotland) with 'ONE POUND' underneath – 1984 and 1989.
3. A leek inside a coronet (for Wales) with 'ONE POUND' underneath – 1985 and 1990.
4. A flax plant inside a coronet (For Northern Ireland) with 'ONE POUND' underneath – 1986 and 1991.
5. An oak tree inside a coronet (for England) with 'ONE POUND' underneath – 1987 and 1992.
6. A set of arms within a crowned shield with 'ONE POUND' underneath – 1988.
7. A lion rampant within an ornate border (for Scotland) with 'ONE POUND' underneath outside the border – 1994 and 1999.
8. A dragon (for Wales) with 'ONE POUND' underneath – 1995.
9. A Celtic cross with a central pimpernel (for Northern Ireland) with 'ONE POUND' underneath – 1996.
10. Three lions (for England) one on top of the other with 'ONE POUND' underneath – 1997.

Edge: Milled with incuse inscriptions according to the country represented on the reverse:

1. 'DECUS ET TUTAMEN' – 1983, 1986, 1987, 1988, 1991, 1992, 1993, 1996, 1997 and 1998.
2. 'NEMO ME IMPUNE LACESSIT' – 1984, 1989, 1994 and 1999.
3. 'PLEIDOL WYF I'M GWLAD' – 1985, 1990, 1995.

Years Produced:

The descriptions of the obverses, reverses and edges precisely define which coins were struck in which year and are not repeated here, except to say that business strikes were produced for each year up to and including 1997. All years were struck for the brilliant uncirculated and proof sets.

Varieties:

Generically, edge inscriptions may be the correct way up or upside down, when the obverse is placed on a flat surface, face up. Since the lettering is pressed into the edge prior to striking, these types are about equally common, but can be regarded as varieties. Thus each year has two types.

Other than these generic types, there are just two years where varieties have been identified: 1985 and 1986.

Care is needed with this series since there are many examples in circulation with errors where the wrong obverse/reverse pairs occur. These are virtually all forgeries and not genuine varieties.

1985 Business Strike Pound:

The 1985 business strike pound has the standard obverse and reverse with no variation, but in a few cases, specimens show an error in the edge lettering, where there is a missing ' in 'I'M'. This is known on a number of coins, but may still be the result of careless forgery, rather than a genuine striking error, or perhaps through the accumulation of grease in the die used.

1986 Business Strike Pound:

Major Varieties:

The 1986 Northern Ireland flax plant pound coin has the standard second decimal obverse bust (obverse 1), but is found with one of two reverses (reverses A and B), giving the die pairings 1+A and 1+B.

Reverse A:

- Larger border beads.
- Beads closer to the rim.
- The tips of the roots of the plant are pronounced.
- The 'P' of 'POUND' points to a space between beads.
- The left leg o the 'N' in 'POUND' points to left of a bead.
- The right leg o the 'N' in 'POUND' points to a space.
- The upright of the 'D' in 'POUND' points to right of a bead.
- The 'E' of 'ONE' points to a space.

Reverse B:

- Smaller border beads.
- Beads away from the rim.
- The tips of the plant roots are less well defined.
- The 'P' of 'POUND' points to a border bead.
- The left leg of the 'N' in 'POUND' points to right of a bead.
- The right leg of the 'N' in 'POUND' points to a bead.
- The upright of the 'D' in 'POUND' points to left of a bead.
- The 'E' of 'ONE' points to a bead.

The reverse A type is present in the BU and proof sets, whilst both types are about equally common amongst circulating coins.

Figure 246 – 1986 Business Strike One Pound Reverses (1)

Reverse A	**Reverse B**
Larger border beads	Smaller border beads
Beads closer to rim	Beads away from rim

Figure 247 – 1986 Business Strike One Pound Reverses (2)

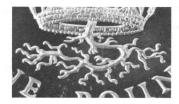 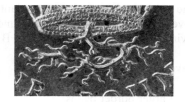

Reverse A	**Reverse B**
Plant roots tips well defined	Plant root tips less well defined

Figure 248 – 1986 Business Strike One Pound Reverses (3)

Reverse A	**Reverse B**
'P' points to a space	'P' points to a bead
1st leg of 'N' to left of bead	1st leg of 'N' to right of bead
2nd leg of 'N' to a space	2nd leg of 'N' to a bead
'D' points to right of bead	'D' points to left of bead

Figure 249 – 1986 Business Strike One Pound Reverses (4)

Reverse A	**Reverse B**
'E' points to a space	'E' points to a bead

228

Minor Varieties:

There are no reported minor varieties for the 1986 pound coin.

*   *   *   *   *

Denomination: Two Pounds

1986-96	1997	1998-99

1986	1989	1989	1994

1995	1995	1996

1997-1999	1999

Specification: Diameter: 28.4mm
Weight: 15.98g (Nickel-brass)
           12.0g (Bimetallic)
Metal: Nickel-brass (1986 – 1996)
           Bimetallic (1997 – 1999) and to date

Obverse Designs:

Elizabeth's bust facing right with the legend:

1. '·ELIZABETH·II·DEI·GRATIA·REGINA·F·D·TWO POUNDS' – 1986 – 1996

230

2. 'ELIZABETH·II·DEI·GRATIA·REGINA·F·D' – 1997
3. 'ELIZABETH·II·DEI·GRA·REG·FID·DEF ·' – 1998 – 1999 (and to date)

The first two pound coin was minted in 1986 as a commemorative for the Commonwealth Games and used the then current decimal bust as designed by Raphael David Maklouf, and found on all other denominations for this date. This second decimal effigy was used until 1997 after which the third decimal bust (fourth bust of the Queen's reign) designed by Ian Rank-Broadley was introduced.

Reverse Designs:

1. A thistle on a St Andrew's cross and the date 1986 across the top – 1986.
2. An intertwined 'W' and 'M' for William and Mary threaded around a horizontal mace and topped with a crown, and with the dates 1689 above 1989 below. The inscription 'TERCENTENARY OF THE BILL OF RIGHTS' around the coin – 1989.
3. An intertwined 'W' and 'M' for William and Mary threaded around a horizontal mace and topped with the crown of Scotland, and with the dates 1689 above 1989 below. The inscription 'TERCENTENARY OF THE CLAIM OF RIGHTS' around the coin – 1989.
4. A central seal of the Bank of England, topped by an interlinked 'W' and 'M' for William and Mary, itself topped by a crown. The seal is flanked by the dates '1694' and '1994' and the inscription 'Bank of England' around the bottom – 1994.
5. A stylised dove carrying an olive branch to commemorate the 50th anniversary of the end of WW II – 1995.
6. A series of flags emanating from the UN 50 logo, which is partially circled by a large '5' and an interlinked '0'. Around the top of the coin is the inscription 'NATIONS UNITED FOR PEACE' and around the bottom, the dates '1945 – 1995' – 1995.
7. A stylised football carrying the date (1996) on one panel and with 16 small circles representing the final 16 of the Euro 96 Championships – 1996.
8. The first currency issue of a bi-metallic two pound coin. The design features a series of rings depicting various stages of development of man, starting at the Iron Age in the centre and working outwards through the cogs of the industrial revolution to the electronic age of silicon chips. The final brass outer ring depicts the internet age with 'TWO POUNDS' around the top and the date around the bottom – 1997-date.
9. A symbolic representation of a Rugby stadium with a rugby ball and goalposts, and '1999' across the top plus 'TWO POUNDS' around the bottom. Designed for the rugby world cup – 1999.

Edge: Milled with incuse inscriptions:

1. 'XIII COMMONWEALTH GAMES SCOTLAND 1986' – 1986.
2. Milled, no inscription – 1989 (both types), 1995 (UN).
3. 'SIC VOS NON VOBIS' – 1994
4. '1945 IN PEACE GOODWILL 1995' – 1995 (Dove)
5. 'TENTH EUROPEAN CHAMPIONSHIP' – 1996
6. 'STANDING ON THE SHOULDERS OF GIANTS' – 1997 to date.

7. 'RUGBY WORLD CUP 1999' – 1999.

Years Produced:

The descriptions of the obverses, reverses and edges precisely define which coins were struck in which year and are not repeated here, except to say that business strikes were first produced in 1997 and have continued to be issued to date, alongside commemoratives which have also been issued for circulation. As for other denominations, the Royal Mint produced both uncirculated and proof sets each year and both contain the standard issue two pound coins for that year. For 1997 and 1998 these are the bimetallic 'Ages of Man' coins, whereas for 1999 the 'rugby world cup' coin is included.

Varieties:

There are no reported varieties of any date in this series. However, like the pound coins, the edge inscriptions may be the correct way up or upside down when the coin is placed on a table obverse up.

*　　*　　*　　*　　*

Denomination: Five Pounds

1990

1993

1996

1997

1998 – 1999

1990

1993

1996

1997

1998

1999   1999

Specification: Diameter: 38.6mm
       Weight: 28.3g
       Metal: Cupro-nickel (75% Copper/25% nickel)

Obverse Designs:

Elizabeth's bust facing right with the legend:

1. 'ELIZABETH·II·DEI·GRATIA·REGINA·F·D·FIVE POUNDS·' – 1990, 1996 (second decimal bust).
2. 'ELIZABETH·II·D·G·REG·F·D·Date' – 1998 – 1999 (and to date) (third decimal bust).
3. Elizabeth's first bust (small) facing right, inside a circle surrounded by mounted trumpeters separated by sceptres and swords and the inscription 'ELIZABETH II DEI·GRATIA·REGINA·FID·DEF·FIVE POUNDS·' around the outside - 1993.
4. Conjoined busts of Philip and Elizabeth facing right and with the legend 'ELIZABETH·II·D·G·REG·F·D PHILIP·PRINCEPES'.

The first five pound coin was minted in 1990 to commemorate the 90th birthday of the Queen Mother, the obverse being the then current decimal bust as designed by Raphael David Maklouf, and found on all other denominations for this date. This second decimal effigy was used on the 1996 coin, then in 1998 the third decimal bust (fourth bust of the Queen's reign) designed by Ian Rank-Broadley was introduced. The 1993 coin is interesting as the Queen's effigy used is the first bust from the pre-decimal era by Mary Gillick, the overall design being by Robert Elderton. Finally, the 1997 coin was designed by Philip Nathan and, for the first time since William and Mary used conjoined busts for the obverse.

All the five pound coins were minted as commemoratives rather than circulating coins.

Reverse Designs:

1. Two 'Es' intertwined, with a crown on top with a rose and thistle to either side, and with the inscription 'QUEEN ELIZABETH THE QUEEN MOTHER 1900 1990' around the outside. Designed by Leslie Durban – 1990.
2. Designed by Robert Elderton, a crown within a circle with 40 radiating trumpets

234

extending outwards and the inscription 'FAITH AND TRUTH I WILL BEAR UNTO THEE'. Produced to commemorate the 40th anniversary of the Queen's coronation – 1993.

3. Designed by Avril Vaughan, the Queen's personal flag, the Union Flag, the Royal Standard and two other pennants bearing the dates 1926 and 1996, all against the background of Windsor castle. Produced to commemorate the Queen's 70th birthday – 1996.

4. Designed by Leslie Durban, the arms of the Royal Couple with a crown above and an anchor below. The dates 1947 and 1997 around the top, '20 NOVEMBER' atop the shields and 'FIVE POUNDS' around the bottom. Struck to commemorate the royal wedding – 1997.

5. Designed by Michael Noakes, a portrait of Prince Charles facing front right towards a banner proclaiming 'THE PRINCE'S TRUST'. Around the top of the coin the words 'FIFTIETH BIRTHDAY OF H·R·H THE PRINCE OF WALES' and around the bottom, '1948 FIVE POUNDS 1998' – 1998.

6. A portrait of Princess Diana facing right, with the dates 1961 above 1997 and the inscription 'IN MEMORY OF DIANA PRINCESS OF WALES·FIVE POUNDS·'. Designed by David Cornell to commemorate the death of Diana – 1999.

7. A stylised clock face with the hands at midnight and passing through the Greenwich Meridium in the British Isles. The words 'ANNO DOMINI' on the clock face and '1999' to the top left, '2000' to the top right and 'FIVE POUNDS' around the bottom. Designed by Jeffrey Matthews to commemorate the new millennium – 1999.

Edge: Milled with incuse inscriptions:

1. Plain milled – 1990, 1993, 1997, 1998 and 1999 (Diana).
2. Incuse 'VIVAT REGINA ELIZABETHA' – 1996.
3. Incuse 'WHAT'S PAST IS PROLOGUE' – 1999 (Millenium).

Years Produced:

The descriptions of the obverses, reverses and edges precisely define which coins were struck in which year and are not repeated here. As for other denominations, the Royal Mint produced both uncirculated and proof strikes for these coins each year and these are contained in the sets as well as in individual card holders.

Varieties:

There are no reported varieties of any date in this series.

* * * * *

And Finally:

As in my previous book, covering the bronze coins of the 20th century, I am conscious that my descriptions of the varieties for the decimal coinage only cover the period from its introduction in 1971 up to the early 1980s and there is very little known for the late 1980s and 1990s. I suspect that this is because the studies that have been made were mostly carried out by the mid 1980s and since then there have been no similar studies of later coins. Perhaps these have been done and, because of modern minting methods, no varieties have been found, or maybe the coins are of low interest to collectors and, therefore, there has been little incentive to undertake this job. From experience I can say that the study of large numbers of similar coins can be an extremely tedious business so I can well understand why nobody has taken on such a task.

So, if anyone reading this feels the overwhelming need for a place in numismatic history, then I suggest that this might be assured by undertaking a study of the cupronickel coins from around 1984 up to 2008, thus achieving the status of expert in this field in the numismatic world. After all you would be following in the steps of the greats like Spink, Peck, Freeman, Davies, Rayner, Seaby and.........Groom!

As I have said earlier in the introduction to this book, if anybody does undertake this work or is aware of publications where it is recorded then please let me know as I will then be able to record the details (and the acknowledgments) in a future edition of this book. Similarly, if I have missed any types from the pre-decimal series, then I would also be grateful for advice about them for future inclusion.

*   *   *   *   *

APPENDIX 1

AUTHOR CONTACT DETAILS

Mobile: 07957 432896

Email: ukc801988231@btconnect.com

APPENDIX 2

BIBLIOGRAPHY

1. Peter J Davies, *British Silver Coins Since 1816,* 1st Edition, 1982, Copyright Peter Davies.
2. *Coins Market Values 1973*, Link House Publications, 1972.
3. Chris Henry Perkins, *Collectors Coins GB 2007,* 34th Edition, Rotographic Publications.
4. R J Marles, *Collectors Coins GB 1998,* 25th Edition, Rotographic Publications
5. Philip Skingley, *Standard Catalogue of British Coins, Coins of England and the United Kingdom*, 39th Edition, Spink, London.
6. Mark Davidson and Allan Hailstone, *Coincraft's Standard Catalogue of English and UK Coins 1066 to Date*, 1997, Standard Catalogue Publishers Ltd for Coincraft.
7. Michael G Salzman, *A Handbook of Modern British Coins and Their Varieties 1797-1970*, First Edition, 1982, Books for Dillons Only.
8. Chris Henry Perkins and Scott D Simon, *Check Your Change,* 5th Edition 2007, Rotographic International.
9. Michael Gouby, Michael Coins website: http://www.michael-coins.co.uk/
10. A. J. Braybrook, *Coin Monthly, Volume 5, Number 4, Page 44, Coin Varieties – Threepences, sixpences & shillings,* 1971, Numismatic Publishing Company.
11. A. J. Braybrook, *Coin Monthly, Volume 5, Number 5, Page 38, Coin Varieties – florin, halfcrown, crown and decimal,* 1971, Numismatic Publishing Company.
12. D. H. Perrin, *Coin Monthly, Volume 5, Number 8, Page 67, 20C Coin Varieties – sixpences, shillings, florins & 10p,* 1971, Numismatic Publishing Company.
13. D. H. Perrin, *Coin Monthly, Volume 5, Number 9, Page 37, 20C Coin Varieties – halfcrowns, 50p and crowns,* 1971, Numismatic Publishing Company.
14. D. M. Beecham, *Coin Monthly, Volume 6, Number 3, Page 25, Halfcrown Varieties,* 1972, Numismatic Publishing Company.
15. J. C. Rudge, *Coin Monthly, Volume 12, Number 2, Page 31,The 19 Varieties of the 1949 Shilling,* December 1977, Numismatic Publishing Company.
16. A. W. Bacon, *Coin Monthly, Volume 12, Number 8, Page 6, Elizabeth II Cupro-Nickel Varieties, June 1978*, Numismatic Publishing Company.
17. A. W. Bacon, *Coin Monthly, Volume 12, Number 9, Page 6, Elizabeth II Cupro-Nickel Varieties, July 1978*, Numismatic Publishing Company.
18. Ron Stafford, *Coin Monthly, Volume 17, Number 5, Page 88, Varieties of the Halfcrown 1816-1967, September 1982*, Numismatic Publishing Company.
19. Ron Stafford, *Coin Monthly, Volume 17, Number 6, Page 76, Varieties of the Halfcrown 1816-1967, October 1982*, Numismatic Publishing Company.
20. E B Mackenzie, *Coin Monthly, The Shillings of 1920 & 1921, February 1983*, Numismatic Publishing Company.
21. E B Mackenzie, *Coin Monthly, Page 89 Shilling Variations of Three Reigns, July 1983*, Numismatic Publishing Company.
22. Ron Stafford, *Coin Monthly, Page 21, Varieties of the Florin 1887-1952, November 1983*, Numismatic Publishing Company.
23. Ron Stafford, *Coin Monthly, Page 5, Latest Discoveries, January 1984*, Numismatic Publishing Company.
24. Chris Henry Perkins, Scott D Simon, *Check Your Change,* 5th Edition, 2007, Rotographic International.

BIBLIOGRAPHY (Cont)

25. K.B. Wiles and E.B.Mackenzie, *Coin Monthly, Volume 10, Number 6, Page 6, 10 Pence Decimal Varieties, April 1976*, Numismatic Publishing Company.
26. K.B. Wiles and E.B.Mackenzie, *Coin Monthly, Volume 10, Number 7, Page 52, 10 Pence Decimal Varieties, May 1976*, Numismatic Publishing Company.
27. News round-up, *Coin Monthly, Volume 11, Number 7, Page 122, 10 Pence Mis-strike, May 1977*, Numismatic Publishing Company.
28. J. C. Rudge, *Coin Monthly, Volume 12, Number 5, Page 51, Milling Variations in Modern Halfcrowns, March 1978*, Numismatic Publishing Company.
29. J. C. Rudge, *Coin Monthly, Volume 13, Number 2, Page 61, Milling Variations in Modern Sixpences, December 1978*, Numismatic Publishing Company.
30. K.B. Wiles and E.B.Mackenzie, *Coin Monthly, Volume 12, Number 11, Page 6, 10 Pence Decimal Varieties, September 1978*, Numismatic Publishing Company.
31. K.B. Wiles and E.B.Mackenzie, *Coin Monthly, Volume 13, Number 1, Page 43, Letters to the Editor, November 1978*, Numismatic Publishing Company.
32. Ron Stafford, *Coin Monthly, Volume 13, Number 4, Page 6, 20,000 Florins. A survey of circulating coins, February 1979*, Numismatic Publishing Company.
33. E.B.Mackenzie, Ron Stafford, *Coin Monthly, Volume 13, Number 5, Page 43, Letters to the editor, March 1979*, Numismatic Publishing Company.
34. Flt Lt P.S.Mackenzie, *Coin Monthly, Volume 13, Number 7, Page 55, Letters to the editor, May 1979*, Numismatic Publishing Company.
35. Ron Stafford, *Coin Monthly, Page 75, Varieties of the Florin Part 3 – Elizabeth II, December 1983*, Numismatic Publishing Company.
36. Ron Stafford, *Coin Monthly, Page 5, Latest Discoveries, January 1984*, Numismatic Publishing Company.
37. D Gimes, *Coin Monthly, Page 49, Letters to the Editor, October 1978*, Numismatic Publishing Company.
38. Ron Stafford, *Coin Monthly, Page 64, Coin Varieties: Latest Discoveries, July 1987*, Numismatic Publishing Company.
39. Ron Stafford, *Coin Monthly, Page 43, Coin Varieties: Latest Discoveries, August 1987*, Numismatic Publishing Company.
40. David Sealy, *Coins and Medals, Page 39, Coin Varieties, July 1970*, Token Publishing Limited.
41. Ron Stafford, *Coin Monthly, Page 66, Coin Varieties: Latest Discoveries, October 1987*, Numismatic Publishing Company.
42. E. B. Mackenzie, *Coin Monthly, Page 9, Proof Decimal Variations in the 10p piece, 7 Mar – 20 Mar 1980*, Numismatic Publishing Company.

APPENDIX 3 – 10p Variety Correlation Chart

YEAR	DAVIES – 1982	STAFFORD 1st – 2/79	STAFFORD 2nd – 12/83	WILES & MACKENZIE 1st – 5/76	WILES & MACKENZIE 2nd – 9/78
1968	1A	1A	1A	1A	1A
	2A	2A	2A	2A	2A
	2B	2B	2B	2B	2B
	3A	3A	2A sub type	3A	3A
	3B	3B	2B sub type	3B	3B
1969	2B	N/K	N/K	N/K	N/K
	3B	4B	2B	4B	4B
		5B		5B	5B
		6B		6B	6B
1970	4B	7B	3B	7B	7B
	4F		3C		7F
1971	4B	8B	3B	8B	8B
1973	3B	11B	2B	11B	11B
	3C	11C	2E		11C
	4B	9B	3B	9B	9B
		10B		10B	10B
	5B	12B	5B	12B	12B
	5C	12C	5E	12C	12C
	6D	13D	4D	13D	13D
1974	3B	11B	2B	11B	11B
1975	4E	9E	3F	9B	9E
	4B	9B	3B		9B
		10B		10B	10B
1976	7B	14B	2B	N/R	14B
	7E	14E	2F		14E
1977	3B	15B	2B	N/R	4B
1971 PROOF	4B	N/R	3B PROOF	N/R	P8B
1972 PROOF	7B	N/R	2B PROOF	N/R	P15B
	7E		2F PROOF		P15E
1973 PROOF	3B	N/R	2B PROOF	N/R	P11B
	3E		2F PROOF		P11E
	9E		6F PROOF		P17E
1974 PROOF	7B	N/R	2B PROOF	N/R	P15B
	7E		2F PROOF		
1975 PROOF	4B	N/R	3B PROOF	N/R	P8B
	4E		3F PROOF		P8E
1976 PROOF	7B	N/R	2B PROOF	N/R	P15B
	7E		2F PROOF		P15E
1977 PROOF	8E	N/R	7F PROOF	N/R	P16E
	10E		8F PROOF		P18E

241

NOTES:

1. In the chart N/K = Not known. This relates to the 1969 ten pence with obverse 2 which is not mentioned by any other sources.
2. In the chart, N/R = Not Reported, generally because of the date of the report versus the date of the coin.
3. The two studies carried out by Wiles and Mackenzie were reported in 5/76 and 9/78, whilst those of R. Stafford were later in 2/79 and 12/83.
4. The correlations with Wiles and Mackenzie in 9/78 are not precisely as reported at the time, but also include further changes made later and interpreted by R. Stafford in 12/83.

DID2490201

L - #0050 - 090419 - C0 - 234/156/13 - PB - DID2490201